CHRIS SIDWELLS is a freelance author and editor who has written well over 1,000 features for magazines and websites including *Cycling Weekly, Cycle Sport, Cycling Active, Cycling Fitness, Tour* magazine, *Bicycling, Eroica Britannia, Cycling Plus, Bicycling, GQ* magazine, *The Roar, Men's Fitness, Running Fitness, The Guardian,* the *Independent, The Sunday Times* and the BBC. He is the author of twenty-five books about cycling and has contributed to ten others.

Chris's latest project is Cycling Legends –
www.cyclinglegends.co.uk

GREAT BRITISH CYCLING LEGENDS

Chris Sidwells

AD LIB

First published in the UK in 2023 by
Ad Lib Publishers Ltd
15 Church Road
London SW13 9HE
www.adlibpublishers.com

Text © 2023 Chris Sidwells

Hardback ISBN 9781802471052
eBook ISBN 9781802471687

All rights reserved. No part of this publication may be reproduced in any form or by any means – electronic, mechanical, photocopying, recording or otherwise – or stored in any retrieval system of any nature without prior written permission from the copyright-holders. Chris Sidwells has asserted his moral right to be identified as the author of this work in accordance with the Copyright, Designs and Patents Act of 1988.

A CIP catalogue record for this book is available from the British Library.

Every reasonable effort has been made to trace copyright-holders of material reproduced in this book, but if any have been inadvertently overlooked the publishers would be glad to hear from them.

Design and typesetting by Danny Lyle

Printed in the UK
10 9 8 7 6 5 4 3 2 1

Contents

Introduction　vii

Chapter 1 The Victorians　1
Chapter 2 Champions and Adventurers　15
Chapter 3 Pioneering Women　45
Chapter 4 Breaking New Ground　57
Chapter 5 Seventies' Flare　83
Chapter 6 The Second Wave　107
Chapter 7 The Off-Roaders　147
Chapter 8 Time of Change　157
Chapter 9 The Golden Years　191
Chapter 10 The Wheel Keeps On Turning　219

List of Legends　243
Picture credits　245

To all British Cycling Legends

Introduction

The last fifteen to twenty years have seen incredible successes for British cyclists in almost every aspect of the sport. Olympic gold medals, world titles, big races, even the biggest race of them all, the Tour de France, have all been won by British cyclists. They have established themselves as legends of the sport and some are household names, legends of all British sport. This book tells their story.

But the book is not limited to recent times, because there were British cycling legends long before. World champions, Olympic medallists, winners of road race classics. It's just that British cycling is different now. The sport changed in the UK at the beginning of the twenty-first century. This book also tells the stories of those who raced before.

The change was slow at first, but quickly became profound. Towards the end of the 1990s, British Cycling, the governing body of cycle racing in the UK, was one of many British sports bodies given access to funding from the national lottery. Before then, most governing bodies survived on income they could generate, which was never consistently enough to support and develop all international competitors so they reached their performance potential.

Of course, some still did reach their potential and they stand out in their sports. Cyclists were no different. Earlier British cycling legends followed their own way, often leaving home to live in a

Introduction

foreign country so they could access competition they needed to improve. It was a real battle at times, but they won through.

Other legends pushed back the frontiers of what cyclists could do, and female cyclists worked to change minds to ensure women got the same opportunities as men to compete. In many ways the legends of yesterday were all pioneers, but that doesn't make their stories more interesting than those of successful cyclists who came later.

Cycling continues to develop as a sport, and British cyclists are still very much part of that. However, with a book like this, which is essentially history, we need a cut-off time. There are many young British cyclists today who are making their own legends; some have already created one, but they have more to add. The final chapter tells the story of four legends who are still racing, but nearing the end of their careers.

All the stories in this book concern remarkable individuals who made their achievements through dedication, discipline, drive and determination. Those are qualities all successful cyclists have, no matter what generation they come from. Individuals express those qualities in different ways, but that only adds to their stories. I hope you enjoy reading them.

Chris Sidwells
April 2023

Chapter One
The Victorians

The bicycle is a nineteenth-century invention, but I believe the first actual bicycle, one with pedals and cranks, was made in France. Many of the first bicycle races were held in France, but British cyclists won many of them, including some of the very first. British cyclists continued winning big European races until the late part of the century, but then an unfortunate accident happened during a British road race, and for a while this country became a road-racing backwater. The country still had some legendary cyclists, mostly in track cycling, but only a few adventurous road racers competed outside the British Isles.

James Moore
14 January 1849 - 17 July 1935
The father of British racing cyclists

James Moore (right), winner of Paris-Rouen, 1869

James Moore was born in Long Brackland, near Bury St Edmonds in Suffolk, the son of blacksmith who was also called James. When James junior was four he moved with his family to Paris, where his father had found better paid work. In the French capital the Moores became acquainted with the Micheaux family, who lived opposite them and who were also blacksmiths.

Either Pierre or Ernest Michaux – there are conflicting stories as to which of the two brothers it was – have both been credited with being the first person to attach cranks and pedals to a wooden, two-wheeled running machine called a draisine, a machine invented in Paris by a German, Baron Karl Friedrich Drais von Sauerbronn in 1817. Draisines could be steered, they had saddles, but were propelled by their riders' feet scooting them along the ground, rather like the balance bike many children learn to cycle on now. In the UK, draisines were called hobby horses.

By inventing a pedalled two-wheel machine, whichever Michaux brother did it had effectively invented cycling. He called his bicycle a *vélocipède*, the shortened version of which, *vélo*, is still the most commonly used French word for bicycle. Michaux's invention caught on quickly, and the family business began mass-producing them. Several other European and UK manufacturers soon began producing their own versions. In the UK these pedal-propelled wooden bikes – with iron bands around their wheels acting as tyres preventing wear from the roads and tracks – were called boneshakers (because they were extremely uncomfortable to ride).

James Moore junior got hold of a Michaux *vélocipède* in 1865 and loved riding it around the streets of Paris, often visiting Cirque d'Eté, a permanent circus, where he was taught to perform tricks on his bike. Three years after that, and with a good few cycling miles in his legs, Moore took part in a race held in the Parc de St Cloud, in Paris. For many years it was thought to be the first-ever bicycle race, although there were other races before, but more has been written about St Cloud. James Moore won, and the bike he won it on is displayed in a museum in Ely, Suffolk.

The next big milestone in cycle racing history was the first long-distance race on public roads (as opposed to races being held in parks or around running tracks, or very short races on public roads). It was organised by another French bike manufacturing family, the Olivier brothers, and ran from Paris to Rouen, a distance of 81 miles (130 km).

Paris to Rouen (note that place-to-place races in cycling are referred to with a hyphen replacing the word 'to', so Paris-Rouen) was held on 7 November 1869. Thirty-two competitors – thirty-one men and one woman, assembled at 7.15 a.m. outside a former exhibition centre, now a famous restaurant, the Le Pré Catalan on the Route de Suresnes in the Bois de Boulogne. They set off in darkness ten minutes later, heading for Rouen.

A fine drizzle fell all day, and it was dark again when Moore arrived at the finish line in Rouen after more than thirteen hours of pedalling his heavy bike along appalling country roads. Roads that in those days were constructed and maintained for horses, not bicycles. Moore often had to dismount and push his bike through axle-deep mud, and he was forced to walk up the hills, but finished fifteen minutes ahead of the next rider.

The bike he rode was constructed from steel rather than wood, and had ball bearings, invented by the bike's manufacturer, Suriray, a business that used prisoners to polish the bearings for their bikes. It also had solid rubber tyres, so it wasn't as bone-jarring as the original wooden boneshakers and *vélocipèdes*, but still must have been very uncomfortable to ride.

The Franco-Prussian War in 1870 stopped cycle racing for a while and then Moore carried on winning, racing on both sides of the Channel. He was one of the first cyclists to set a record for how much distance he could cover in one hour, (now called the Hour Record), completing 14 miles and 880 yards in sixty minutes at the Molyneux Grounds in Wolverhampton. Moore also won the MacGregor Cup, which was regarded as a series of unofficial world cycling championships, from 1872 to 1875 and again in 1877. He ended his cycle racing career shortly after that last victory to pursue his other vocation.

Moore had become familiar with horses through his father's work, and the animals became a lifelong passion. When he stopped racing he studied to be a vet, practising in France once he qualified, eventually setting up a stud farm in Normandy. Even though he spent the majority of his life as a vet and working with horses, James Moore is still remembered as the father of British cycle racing.

David Stanton

11 July 1844 – date unknown
Winner of the first ever six-day cycle race

The front cover of *The Pictorial World* from 30 November 1878 showing David Stanton, top left

From the first such event, held in London's Agricultural Hall, Islington, right up until the late 1980s, six-day cycle racing was a very popular part of the sport. Held during each winter in indoor velodromes, six-day races were watched by capacity crowds all over Europe, and during the first half of the twentieth century in North America as well. However, the racing those later European and American crowds watched was very different to the first ever six-day race.

It was won by a Welshman, David Stanton, who was a gambler by profession. In his late twenties he discovered that he could ride a 'high-wheeler' bike, or 'penny-farthing' as they are more often referred to now. And not only could he ride one quickly, he could ride for very long distances. He also found out he could make money from it.

Stanton began competing in 1873, and if he thought he could win a race he would back himself with bookmakers who were at every track meeting in those days. The tracks Stanton competed on were flat, very like athletics tracks, and they were all outdoors. Between 1873 and 1876 Stanton won or was placed top three in many long-distance bike races that were part of big track meetings held all over the UK. His fame spread and in 1877 he was invited to take part in an eighty-kilometre track race in New York, which he won.

For his next wager, David Stanton chose an indoor venue. In 1878 he bet a number of wealthy gentlemen he could ride a thousand miles within six days, six being chosen due to a ban on gambling on Sundays in Victorian England.

A flat, vaguely oval track was marked out inside the Agricultural Hall, Islington, which is still there today, and Stanton rode his penny-farthing around it, lap after lap after lap. He competed 172 miles the first day, Monday and 160 on each subsequent day, eating and sleeping between sessions on the bike. Finally, with just twenty-seven minutes of Saturday night to go, Stanton completed a thousand miles.

It was quite a feat: he rode for 73.5 of the 144 hours, giving an average speed of 13.5 miles per hour. That was some performance on a Victorian bike with one big wheel (the 'penny') and one small one (the 'farthing', the back wheel), pedalled around and around in circles.

Now, watching that might not appeal nowadays, but Victorian Londoners loved it. Thousands attended throughout Stanton's riding hours, lost in admiration for his endurance and bravery. Another six-day race was put on at the same venue a few months later, only this time it was a race between several competitors on bikes and one riding a horse – well, several horses, actually. The competition was weighted heavily in favour of four legs as well, because the horse rider, a Mexican, was allowed to change horses and ride another while the horse he had been riding was rested.

But despite things being stacked in their favour the horses didn't get as far as Stanton, completing only 969 miles in 144 hours, although the first of the latest batch of cyclists was still 59 miles behind them. It was another big hit, though, and six-day racing became a thing. The next London six-day race, also in 1878, had ten cyclists and no horses. The field included a French racer who was a star in his own country, Charles Terront, but the race was won by William Cann from Sheffield, who rode 1,060.5 miles and won a hundred pounds.

The Victorians

People soon became hooked on watching six-day races, and 1879 saw several of them in the UK and in the US. The London six-day of that year was billed as the world championships of six-day racing. A cyclist from Newcastle, George Waller, won with a total of 1,172 miles ridden in the six days. David Stanton was fourth.

Other British cities hosted six-days and the fashion spread throughout Europe and the US. In November 1879, Stanton won the Chicago six-day as part of a four-man team with Charles Terront, William Cann and John Keen. The team format was used to make the racing faster and more exciting, and it increased the distances ridden, which attracted even more interested spectators.

Speeds also increased with bicycle development, and six-day racing switched to steeply banked tracks made from wood. They were either prefabricated – so they could be assembled inside a building for a six-day race, then disassembled afterwards – or they were permanent tracks constructed inside custom-made buildings called velodromes. Races were still contested by teams in what was called Madison racing, in which the two riders of a team are on the track one at a time. When the racer wants the other to take over, they physically push them into the race. This type of racing became the heart of six-days. It's also a stand-alone event at the Olympic Games and in track cycling world championships. The race was named after Madison Square Garden in New York, where it was invented.

Over the years six-day racing became a very lucrative offshoot of pro cycling, and the fact that it was invented by a British gambler riding a penny-farthing in circles for a bet is often overlooked. A lot of professional cyclists owe a debt of gratitude to David Stanton.

George Pilkington Mills

8 January 1867 – 8 November 1945
One of the greatest ever
long-distance cyclists

George Pilkington Mills (second from left) with the rest of the English team who took part in the first Bordeaux-Paris race held in 1891

George Pilkington Mills, from Paddington in London, was the supreme long-distance cyclist of his generation. He started cycling at the age of twelve, and early racing flair saw him quickly recruited by the elite Anfield Cycling Club, which contained most of the top long-distance racers in the UK.

In 1885 and still only eighteen, Mills set a new British twenty-four-hour record of 259 miles, riding a penny-farthing. The race he set the record in was called the Anfield Twenty-Four-Hour, and Mills repeated his victory the following year. But an even more remarkable achievement came later in 1886 when he rode a penny-farthing from Land's End to John O'Groats – a route known in cycling as the End To End, just over nine hundred miles in the days before the Forth and Tay road bridges were constructed – in a record time of five days and one hour. It was a real adventure, a ride into the unknown. Many people in the far north of Scotland had never even seen a bicycle, and the roads Mills mastered were just cart tracks.

Just a few days later Mills was back in Land's End again, this time riding a tricycle to John O'Groats, arriving there five days and ten hours later to set a new tricycle End To End record. Mills eventually set six new long-distance records that year, an incredible feat given the primitive state of both the roads and early bicycles. It's one that has never been repeated.

The Victorians

Meanwhile, in France huge interest had grown up around long-distance cycling, and newspapers were competing for readers by trying to organise the longest races. In 1891 a paper called *Le Vélocesport* put on a race between Bordeaux and Paris, 362 miles in one go; there was no such thing as stage racing in those days. Mills took part with three other long-distance record-setters, Montague Holbein, Selwyn Edge and J. E. Bates.

By this time, Mills had joined another elite long-distance club, the North Road Cycling Club, established to promote record setting on the A1, which was then called the Great North Road. The club was also home to Holbein, Edge and Bates. Their reputation was their invition to take part in the Bordeaux-Paris on 24 May 1891.

Thirty-eight competitors started at 5 a.m. from the Pont Bastide in Bordeaux. Most were French and alongside the four from Great Britain, there was also a Swiss rider and a Pole. All but one of them rode Safety Bicycles, a recent development in which the cranks and pedals turned a chain, which drove the rear wheel. These bikes were less dangerous, hence their name, easier to ride and much faster than penny-farthings.

Competitors carried control cards which they stopped to get stamped at checkpoints along the way. At the first stop in Angoulême, all four British riders arrived together with a healthy lead on the rest. Riders could take on extra food and liquids at checkpoints and the four British riders quickly drank some soup before setting off again.

Pacers were allowed to join the race from Angoulême to Paris, and Mills had a pretty fast selection of them lined up to meet him at each checkpoint and lead him to the next. He quickly drew ahead of the whole field, and by the next checkpoint led Holbein by half an hour, with Edge and Bates the next two to arrive.

That was how the race progressed. Mills drew further and further ahead, eventually winning in Paris in a time of 26 hours,

36 minutes and 25 seconds. Holbein was second in 27 hours 52 minutes and Edge was third in 30 hours and 10 minutes. Bates was fourth, just eight seconds behind Edge, leaving the rest of the pack a long way behind.

Mills raced for a few years more and when he stopped he took up a position with the British bike manufacturer Raleigh, redesigning their production system with greater automation. He joined the army in 1889, and retired a major in 1906, but volunteered again during the First World War. He was promoted to lieutenant-colonel, mentioned in dispatches several times, and was awarded the Distinguished Service Order.

Although it's not part of the elite men's racing calendar now, Bordeaux-Paris became regarded as one of the 'Classics', the best single-day races. As well as being one of the greatest long-distance cyclists the sport has ever seen, Mills is also the first British cyclist to have won a Classic race. He's a double British cycling legend.

Frederick Thomas Bidlake

13 March 1867 – 17 September 1933
The father of British time-trialling

The plaque in the garden created in memory of Frederick Thomas Bidlake in Sandy, Bedfordshire

British time trials are a world within cycling, with their own traditions and history dating back to Victorian times. They are still run very much as they were, and held over set distances; twenty-five miles, fifty miles and a hundred miles, plus set times of twelve and twenty-four hours. And for a very long time they were the mainstay of British cycle racing and cycling club life.

They came about in 1894, after the governing body of cycling in the UK, the National Cycling Union (NCU), banned bunched racing on public roads. Trials were the brainchild of Frederick Thomas Bidlake. He was a lifelong cyclist who made his name in competition as a record-breaking trike racer, at one time holding every tricycle record from fifty miles to twenty-four hours, as well as a number of place-to-place records of a body called the Road Records Association (RRA), which he helped to create. The RRA is still very active today and still lives by the same rules – riders set a date for their record attempts and must be solo or tandem.

Bidlake was a natural organiser, and it was as such he made his lasting mark in the history of British cycling. He was an administrator while still an active competitor and had been involved in the incident that provoked the NCU bunched road racing ban.

Bidlake was taking part in a fifty-mile road race just north of London. He was doing well, leading with another competitor,

Arthur Ilsley and their respective pace-makers, when they overtook a horse. Unfortunately, the horse was startled and reared up on its hind legs, which unseated its rider. Thankfully, she was unhurt, but she reported the matter to the police and that presented the NCU with a problem.

The legal right to cycle on public roads had not been fully established at that time and in 1878 there had been a move in Parliament to amend the prevailing Highways Act to ban bikes. The North Road race incident brought the whole question to public attention again, so the NCU decided to make a pre-emptive strike with its ban on bunched racing to see off the threat of Parliament outlawing all cycling on public roads.

The NCU instructed cycling clubs to organise track races or road races on private circuits – such as motor-racing circuits or around the perimeter tracks of airfields. Frederick Thomas Bidlake, believing cyclists had a right to race on public roads, came up with a way to do it. He thought that competitors could inconvenience other road users in groups but if they started individually at one minute intervals and wore very dark clothing that would attract very little attention and certainly cause no inconvenience.

Each competitor in Bidlake's race design was given a start time and told their number, and when they passed the timekeeper at the finish the competitor shouted out the number and the timekeeper subtracted the rider's start time from their finish time to establish who had covered the race route the fastest. The British time trial was born, and the first race under these rules was over fifty miles and organised by the North Road Cycling Club on 5 October 1895.

A few time trials had been organised before that date by the NCU, but the North Road Cycling Club race was the first to be held under Bidlake's rules, which he summarised by saying his races were 'Private and confidential.' They were so private and confidential, in fact, that no races were advertised, just listed in the UK's cycling magazines. No locations or routes were given: there was just a code for each time trial course in the country. The key to that code was printed in the member's handbook of the UK time-trial governing body that Bidlake created. The Road Time Trials Club (RTTC) still runs the majority of time trial events held in the UK today, although under its new name of Cycling Time Trials (CTT).

Bidlake continued running the RTTC until August 1933 when he was hit by a car when cycling in north London. He didn't appear badly injured at the scene and managed to cycle home, but he later lost consciousness and died twenty days later. There is a memorial garden at Girtford Bridge near Dandy, Bedfordshire, and the Bidlake Memorial Prize is awarded annually for meritorious performance by a UK cyclist.

Chapter Two
Champions and Adventurers

This chapter opens with the stories of Britain's first two world champions. One was not only a world champion but consistently one of the best endurance track racers of his generation, who travelled the world, competing on several continents. The other world champion was a great road cyclist who raced more domestically. The next two riders in the chapter were adventurous road racers who wanted to compete at the highest levels in Europe – they saw no reason why their countrymen shouldn't do the same – and in different ways both helped develop road racing in the UK. The chapter ends by looking at the lives of two astonishing record-breakers whose endurance is testament to what men and women could achieve, and where they could go, just by riding a bike.

Jimmy Michael
8 August 1877 – 21 November 1904
Britain's first cycling
world champion

The short figure of Jimmy Michael at the height of his track cycling career

Jimmy Michael was born in Aberaman in the Cynon Valley of South Wales. Interest in cycling grew quickly in the UK towards the end of the nineteenth century and track cycling became a very popular spectator sport with all classes of people. There were tracks with spectator stands in big cities, and in industrial areas nearly every town or village had a grass track, often built around the edges of a cricket pitch, or they had cinder tracks made from compressed crushed shale, the by-product of coal mining and steel manufacture. The number one industry where Jimmy Michael grew up, in the South Wales Valleys, was coal mining.

As a teenager Michael went to as many cycling tracks as he could. He was fascinated by the racing and wanted to emulate the riders he admired. He managed to get himself a second-hand race bike and started competing. He was an instant success, winning the Welsh five-mile and fifty-mile championships on a track in Newport, Gwent, in his first year.

His Welsh titles brought Michael an invitation to race in the Surrey 100, held at the Herne Hill track in South London. Herne Hill Velodrome went on to be the venue for track cycling in the 1948 Olympic Games, and is still important in the sport today. The race was billed as being contested by the 'The cream of the cracks at the hundred-mile distance.' They were best of their day, but

17

Michael beat them. His diminutive figure – he was five feet tall and weighed seven stone and two pounds – lapped the other riders several times to win the Surrey 100 by seven minutes in a time of just 4 hours 19 minutes.

Suddenly Michael was famous, a local champion who had beaten the best in Britain, some of the best endurance racers in the world. He was invited to ride in prestigious track meetings all over Europe, and was paid to do it. Track cycling was a lucrative business for young men in those days, and at the age of eighteen Michael moved to Paris, where another Welshman, the multiple world record-holder Arthur Linton, was based.

Linton took Michael under his wing and introduced his young compatriot to his trainer, 'Choppy' Warburton. Trainers earned money by taking a share of the cash won by their riders. Warburton, a former runner, carried a doctor's bag wherever he went, and there are a number of reports from that time saying he carried substances to revive riders in a state of exhaustion during very long races. They were said to become fully and instantly rejuvenated and carried on to win. The inference being it was very powerful medicine, and he would possibly have been considered to be doping in sport today.

Track cycling has always been divided into sprinters and endurance racers. Michael and Linton were endurance racers, who in their time were referred as stayers. Horse racing had the same division; horses who were fast over short distances were sprinters and those who maintained a slower pace for much longer, who were said to be able to 'stay the distance', were called stayers. Greyhound racing still divides its dogs into sprinters and stayers, using those exact words.

The most popular stayer races were those in which competitors were paced by other racing cyclists riding tandems, triplets with three riders pedalling or other multi-seated bikes powered by four or more pairs of legs. The idea was that more pairs of legs meant more speed and because the competitors sheltered in their pacer's slipstreams they were effectively dragged to the same higher speed.

Pacing increased the spectacle of the race, which drew more people to watch the track meetings. In longer races, paces would be changed with fresh pairs of legs on a new tandem, or whatever multi-rider bike it was, ensuring the race speed stayed high. New tracks were built with hard surfaces and steeply banked bends to prevent the riders flying off the track. Masses of people watched from packed stands at these tracks.

Human-powered pacing was later replaced by motor pacing, with motorbikes of up to 1000 c.c. maintaining average speeds of up to 60 miles per hour in races of a hundred kilometres or more. As you can imagine, the sport became very dangerous, which increased the risk for racers but increased glamour and attraction for spectators.

The riders who took part in the biggest stayer races were all professionals. The first world championships, over the relatively short stayer distance of a hundred kilometres, took place in Cologne in 1885. There had already been two world championships for amateur riders, but professionals were considered cycling's elite by 1885. To make their first world championship race extra special, each competitor was paced by a team of men on two multi-seated bikes; four rode a quadruplet bike, followed by three on a triplet, with the competitor behind the triplet.

What a sight the race must have been for the capacity crowd, who were treated to an epic Jimmy Michael victory. He completed 100 kilometres in 2 hours and 24 minutes, and lapped the second-placed rider twelve times, becoming Britain's first ever world cycling champion.

Track cycling was also big in the US, and after the championships Michael was invited to appear in a series of American track meetings. On his return to Europe he set a new human-paced hour record of 28 miles 1,072 yards, and was in demand at tracks all over the continent, where promoters paid him up to two hundred pounds (something like £16,500 today) to get him in front of as many as twenty thousand paying fans at a single meeting.

Michael became famous on both sides of the Atlantic, earning a great deal of money. He was even painted by Henri Toulouse-Lautrec for an advertising poster. There's a copy of it on display at the National Museum of Wales in Cardiff.

By 1898 Michael was at the height of his popularity and promotors had to pay much more to get him to race at their velodromes. In one series of ten meetings that year, he was paid $2,500 per event. In 1902 Michael raced in Berlin. The track was made from wood and very steeply banked to cope with the increased speed the riders achieved behind motorbikes, but the forces generated by the speed put a huge strain on the pacing motorbikes and the rider's bikes. Michael had averaged nearly 60 miles per hour for the first fifty-eight minutes of the race when the rear wheel of the motorbike pacing him disintegrated. Michael crashed, fracturing his skull – no riders wore safety helmets in those days – and suffered many other injuries.

Jimmy Michael was never the same rider after that terrible crash, and he died in November 1904 aboard a transatlantic liner. Britain's first-ever world cycling champion was buried in Brooklyn, New York, but has never been forgotten in the old mining valleys of Wales.

Dave Marsh

28 December 1894 – 1960
Britain's first road race
world champion

Dave Marsh became the world amateur road champion in August, 1922 in New Brighton, Wallasey

Time trials thrived after their invention by Frederick Thomas Bidlake in 1895, and they produced some very strong riders who set impressive record times, especially when you consider the state of the roads, as well as the heavy unsophisticated bikes they raced on. This British time trialling tradition and strength, as well as a good deal of local knowledge, even helped produce Britain's first road race world champion, a Londoner from Poplar called Dave Marsh.

Marsh was one of four cycling brothers and raced for a number of famous London cycling clubs during his cycling career. He won several national titles, and he was picked for the Great Britain teams for the 1920 and the 1924 Olympic Games. The 1920 Games were held in Antwerp, Belgium, where Marsh was twenty-fourth in the road race. Then four years later they were held in the French capital, Paris, where Marsh was twenty-sixth in the same event.

By the 1920s bunched road racing was a big sport in most countries of continental Europe, with most of the great races we see today already established. However, something about the purity and the 'alone and unaided' ethos of time trialling, where one competitor competes on the race roads with another but cannot shelter behind the other or take any tactical advantage, seemed to impress the organisers of the Olympic Games at that time. They were very much into the Corinthian spirit of sport, so maybe something of the simplicity of time trials appealed, and after a bunched race had decided the road gold medal for the first few modern Olympics, time trials were used to decide it from 1912 until 1932.

Perhaps this led cycling's world governing body, the Union Cycliste Internationale (UCI) to choose a time trial for its inaugural road-race world championships in 1921. Both races were for amateurs, as were the Olympic Games in those days (there was no professional road race in the UCI world championships programme until 1927) and British riders did well in the first, and even better in the second.

The first was held in Copenhagen over a distance of 190 kilometres. The winner was Gunnar Sköld of Sweden, with a Danish rider, Willum Nielson in second place and Charles Davy of Great Britain in third.

The following year the world championships were held in Liverpool, with the road race some way out of the city and following much of the same route at the Anfield Bicycle Club's annual hundred-mile time trial. As an aside, the Anfield club – founded in 1879 – still exists and is one of the oldest cycling clubs in the world. Its hundred-mile time trial is still run annually.

The British team – the previous year's third place Charles Davey, William Burkett and Dave Marsh – all knew the roads well. They dominated, finishing first, second and third; with Marsh winning, Burkett in second and Davey third. Marsh's winning time of 5 hours, 2 minutes and 27 seconds, is a shade under 20 m.p.h. for the 100-miles. The 1921 World Champion, Sköld, was fourth.

It was a great performance, but the following year the UCI road race world championships in Zurich were decided by a bunched race. Marsh was the best British finisher again, but in twenty-fifth position almost 33 minutes behind the winner, was Libero Ferrario of Italy. After that, road race world championships were decided by a bunched race every year, and there wasn't a British men's winner for forty-three years. Why, after such a dominant performance in 1922, was that?

One of the answers is that British riders just weren't used to the cut and thrust of bunched road races. They weren't used to the tactics, weren't familiar with riding in close-quarter groups and lacked the instant changes of pace needed to excel in bunched road racing. With their constant diet of middle and long-distance time trials British road cyclists were fit and strong, they had good endurance and could ride at a good pace all day, but they didn't have the tactical nous to cope with bunched road racing.

Happily, that began to change in the late 1940s and early 1950s, due to the efforts of our next British cycling legend, an irascible, determined man from the Black Country of the English Midlands called Charlie Holland.

Charlie Holland

2 July 1904 – 1 March 1964
First British cyclist to take part in the Tour de France

Charlie Holland in 1937; along with compatriot Bill Burl he would ride the Tour de France. Burl didn't last longer than the first stage, but Holland reached halfway in the race before bad luck put him out

Charlie Holland was born and grew up in the English Midlands. At school he was good at several sports, especially at cricket and football, but his father was a lifelong cyclist who held several local cycling records and wanted his son to race. When Charles was twelve the Holland family started going on long cycle-touring holidays, but Charles didn't actually race until he was eighteen. Five years later he brought home an Olympic bronze medal from the 1932 Los Angeles Games.

The British team pursuit squad for the 1932 Olympics was made up of Holland, Frank Southall, Bill Harvell and Ernie Johnson. All but Johnson also took part in the Olympic road race, run as a time trial. Southall was sixth, Holland fifteenth and Harvell nineteenth. In those days the Olympic road race also had a team classification with its own set of medals, and the British team narrowly missed the bronze.

In 1934 Holland finished fourth in the amateur road race world championships – the delineation between amateurs and professionals would continue almost to the end of the twentieth century. Two years later Holland was selected for the road race at the 1936 Olympic Games in Berlin, where he again just missed out on a medal.

It was a historic Olympics, remembered as much for its celebration of Nazism in Germany as for sport. One day when training with his teammates, Holland passed over on a bridge above an *autobahn*, but he noticed crowds of people lining the motorway below. The British riders stopped, and after a short wait a line of open cars drove beneath them. They contained German political leaders and high-ranking military personal, including Adolf Hitler. Holland often recounted this story in the coming years, saying he could have prevented the Second World War right then by dropping a bomb in Hitler's lap.

In the days when Holland raced there weren't many professional cyclists in the UK. There was no bunched road racing on public roads, only time trials, so the sport in this country was quite separate to cycling in Europe with its Grand Tours, like the Tour de France, and big single-day races. If British amateurs became professionals it was usually at the end of their careers to attack road records, like the Land's End to John O'Groats record. Bike manufacturers paid good money for those riders, as there was huge interest in them among club cyclists, so the record provided great exposure for their bikes.

Holland became a professional cyclist in 1937, but it was to compete in a different type of racing. He wanted to take part in the European six-day track-racing circuit, which was very popular in Europe. Plus it had recently been announced that six-day racing was returning to the UK, with a London six-day held on a track constructed inside the Empire Pool building in Wembley.

Holland would require more track racing experience to take part in six-days, especially experience of racing on the small, steeply banked tracks inside the velodromes of Europe. He moved to Belgium to train and race, but in doing so mixed with Belgian and other European professionals, and heard about the road races they did and in particular about the Tour de France

Holland raced well enough in Belgium to be asked to ride in the 1937 London six-day race, but crashed and broke his collarbone on the first day. By then, though, he really wanted to race in the Tour de France. The Isle of Man allowed road racing on public roads, with all competitors setting off together as opposed to one by one like they do in time trials, and Holland had already won the biggest and best road race on the island.

Holland contacted the newspaper *L'Équipe*, who organised the Tour de France. He presented his CV and the organisers were impressed. Although most competitors in the Tour de France belonged to national or regional teams, it was still possible to enter as an individual. Holland was prepared to do that, but the organisers also had enquiries from another British rider, Bill Burl, and from a Canadian, Pierre Gachon for the 1937 Tour, so all three were invited to take part as the British Empire team, wearing white jerseys with Union Jacks on each sleeve.

Gachon dropped out on day one and Bill Burl was knocked off his bike by an enthusiastic spectator, breaking his collarbone on stage two. Holland continued for several days after that, but he suffered two punctures during a stage through the Pyrenees and, although he had a spare tyre to replace the second, his bicycle pump broke. With race service vehicles well ahead by the time he got round to pumping his new tyre up, and no one around to borrow a working pump from, Holland was forced to stop.

Only forty-six of the ninety-eight starters finished the 1937 Tour, so getting as far as Holland did was a real achievement, but he was sure he could have got further if he hadn't had bad luck and if the race organisation had been more supportive. In an interview many years later Holland said, 'We weren't provided with a manager or any back-up personnel. You cannot look after yourself in a race like the Tour de France. I think the organisers got all the publicity they wanted out of me first, then they didn't want me to finish. How would it have looked if an individual rider with no support had finished their race?'

Holland spent the rest of his cycling career setting new road records, including the London to York record, which he completed in ten hours for the 210 miles, beating the old record by twelve minutes. Two weeks later he set a new record for the 287 miles between Land's End and London, which was twenty-five minutes quicker than the old one.

They are impressive record-breaking margins, but Charlie Holland will always be remembered as the first British cyclist ever to ride the Tour de France, even though he didn't get to the finish. It would be another eighteen years before a British cyclist did that.

Percy Stallard
19 July 1909 – 11 August 2001
The father of British road racing

Percy Stallard, the cyclist who brought bunched road racing to Britain

Percy Stallard was born in Wolverhampton in the West Midlands. He was surrounded by cyclists because his father ran a bike shop in part of their family home. Stallard joined the Wolverhampton Wheelers Cycling Club at the age of sixteen and started competing the following year.

He took part in time trials first, then mixed in some racing on local grass tracks. He also raced on the local banked tracks, of which there were quite a few in the West Midlands. However, Stallard's cycling epiphany came when he took part in a series of bunched races on the Brooklands motor racing circuit in 1933.

The first two road race world championships, in 1921 and 1922, were run as time trials, but in 1923 the championships switched to a bunched race with all competitors starting at the same time. When the Olympic Games reintroduced a road race to its cycling programme in 1936 that too was a bunched race.

UK cycling's governing body at the time, the NCU, only allowed time trials on public roads. British competitors in the 1923 road race world championships found themselves at a disadvantage with no experience of races like it. The pattern continued: British cyclists did OK at world level on the track – Henry Fuller won a bronze medal in the sprint at the 1924 world championships, and Syd Cozens took two silver medals in the same discipline in 1929 and 1930 – but the country was out of its depth in road racing.

In 1933, in an attempt to remedy the situation and give British riders some bunched road race experience, the NCU asked a club local to Brooklands motor racing circuit in Surrey to organise some bunched races. It was a step in the right direction, but motor racing circuits didn't present the same challenges as racing on public roads.

Stallard raced in all the Brooklands events, which the NCU used to select its team for the 1933 road race world championships, and did well enough in the last one to be picked for the British team. The road races were held just outside Paris, coincidentally finishing on the Montlhéry motor racing circuit and Stallard was a creditable eleventh in the amateur world title race.

He still found the changes of pace in bunched road racing difficult to cope with, being more used to the constant effort made in time trials, and felt he lacked the tactical experience to compete as well as he could. Stallard could see no logic in why road racing was banned in the UK, so he started writing letters to the NCU. He didn't get any answers that he felt sufficiently explained why no bunched races were allowed on public roads in the UK.

Stallard was selected for the 1934 road race world championships in Leipzig and improved to seventh place. Then in 1936 he took part in a bunched road race around the famous motorcycle TT circuit on the Isle of Man.

Stallard finished seventeenth in the round-island race, and enjoyed it. It was the first time he'd raced up and down a mountain and through the streets of towns and villages with a whole peloton of riders. The race passed without incident and left Stallard with the absolute certainty that there was no reason why bunched races couldn't be held on the public roads of mainland UK. He increased his efforts to persuade the NCU, but was repeatedly told such races would cause friction with other road users.

Then the Second World War came along and, due to fuel rationing, there was very little traffic on public roads, so Stallard wrote again to the NCU, requesting permission to put on a bunched road race, while pointing out that there would be no friction because very few people were using the roads. He had the backing of the police and local authorities of several councils, which he needed because his race would be between the towns of Llangollen and Wolverhampton, but the NCU still refused to make the race an official event. Stallard went ahead anyway.

A date was set, 7 June 1942, and forty riders joined in, but they couldn't have known they were also joining a conflict with the official body. The race passed without incident. The police helped the marshals and provided motorcycle outriders. Stallard was good at gaining publicity and quite a few spectators turned up to watch the riders go by, with a big crowd at the finish. Albert Price won, a few inches ahead of fellow leading Wolverhampton rider Cecil Anslow, with other finishers stretched out behind them. All were promptly suspended from competition by the NCU, and by the body that governed time trials in the UK, the RTTC. That meant they couldn't compete in any races organised by those two bodies, which back then meant they couldn't compete in any bike race apart from the one they'd just ridden.

Looking back now it's quite amazing this happened, but the NCU's fears about bunched road racing were genuine. The legal right to race bikes on public roads had never been defined, neither had it been contested. The NCU was still worried that bunched road races would disrupt the passage of other road users, attract attention and possible complaints could lead to legislation forbidding all cycling on public roads. But the thing was, the NCU would not even listen to any other view; not to Stallard or anyone else. The governing body would not even take evidence or invite opinion. Instead, they suspended Stallard from competing for life pending an appeal, which he never entered: Percy Stallard was the wrong man to pick a fight with.

He promptly created his own governing body, the British League of Racing Cyclists (BLRC) to run bunched racing on public roads in the UK, and kicked off by organising a national road race championship, which he won. This tore British cycling in half. Lots of club cyclists, especially younger ones, wanted to race in the UK as they could in continental Europe, where cycling was a massive sport; they supported Stallard. But clubs could only affiliate to one organisation, the BLRC or NCU, and even when faced with losing members, the NCU kept suspending any rider who competed in BLRC races.

Battle between the two bodies raged throughout the 1940s and 1950s and the BLRC grew all through that time, establishing road racing in the UK without repercussions from the police or government. The NCU was left with no choice but to broker peace and amalgamate with the BLRC, which it did in 1959. The result was a new body called the British Cycling Federation – today known as British Cycling – which remains the governing body of cycle sport in the UK. All this is due in no small part to the dogged determination of Percy Stallard, the father of British road racing.

Billie Fleming (Dovey)

13 April 1914 – 12 May 2014
A long-time world-record holder who inspired generations of women cyclists

Billie Fleming cycling to a reception in her honour in London, in December, after setting the women's world record of 29,064 miles cycled in one year. It would take seventy-six years for someone to better her achievement

Billie Fleming was born Lillian Irene Bartram in Camden, north London. She left school at sixteen and worked as a typist and secretary and, approaching her eighteenth birthday, took up cycling. She really enjoyed the freedom and feeling of health and fitness. She became a lifelong devotee of exercise – and it was a long life. Billie Fleming lived to see her centenary.

She married Freddie Dovey in 1936, and became involved with the Women's League of Health and Beauty, a mass keep-fit system founded in 1930 by Mary Bagot Stack. They ran classes all over the UK and Billie Dovey saw these as a really accessible way women could gain the benefits of exercise. She wanted to help publicise this new movement and came up with an audacious plan.

She decided to spend a year cycling the length and breadth of Britain, presenting talks and demonstrating exercises, and in doing so boost her fitness so that the people she met would be inspired. She intended to set a record for the number of miles ridden by a female cyclist in one year. There was a men's record, but Billie Dovey was the first woman to make an attempt.

She contacted the manufacturer Rudge-Whitworth, who provided a bike and spares, and Cadbury, who – well, you can guess what Cadbury provided. That was it, no other help, no support crew, but Dovey was a very accomplished cyclist by then. She was also very resourceful.

She started on 1 January 1938 in the north London suburb of Mill Hill, picked because it was where London ended and the A1 became a road through country and not the city. Ratifying records was an entirely do-it-yourself process at that time. Luckily, though, accurate distance measuring devices had been developed for bicycle use. They were called cyclometers, and worked mechanically by counting wheel revolutions and converting the revolutions to distance ridden. Correctly fitted they were quite accurate.

Dovey had her cyclometer tagged and sealed, with a date and time, and fitted by a third party who could testify that they had sealed it, and therefore vouch for the cyclometer's authenticity. She also carried cards and, at a roadside café or wherever she was staying during her round Britain expeditions, another party would write down the date, time and location of the encounter with Billie and sign the card.

She rode her bike every day for a year, eating at transport cafes and sleeping at the homes of those who hosted her fitness talks. She averaged 81.10 miles per day, although did almost two hundred miles on some summer days, and much less in the winter. Her total mileage for the year, and therefore the women's world record, was 29,603.7 miles.

As she progressed towards that amazing mileage figure Billie's ride started attracting media attention. The body adjudicating her record attempt, *Cycling Magazine*, now called *Cycling Weekly*, arranged a big reception when she finished, in London's Agricultural Hall. Billie Dovey was the first woman, certainly the first on record, to have completed a year mileage record, although men had been setting them since 1911 when a Frenchman, Marcel Planes, rode 34,366 miles in a year.

It was a long time before any other woman tried to emulate Dovey, although I am sure she would be thrilled that a woman holds the absolute world year mileage record at the time of writing. She is Amanda Coker, who rode an incredible 86,573.2 miles in 2017, beating the previous male record holder, Kurt Searvogel, by 10,497.2 miles.

Searvogel beat a record set by the next British cycling legend, Tommy Godwin, who rode his 75,065 miles in 1938. It was an incredible distance and incredibly durable, but Dovey's women's world record lasted even longer. It was only broken by Kajsa Tylen as recently as 2016, when she rode 32,526 miles in a year, not that much further than Dovey rode seventy-eight years before her.

Dovey had wanted to set another long-distance record, but her plan to ride across North America in 1939 was thwarted by the outbreak of the Second World War. She did set new records for the fastest tricycle ride over twenty-five, fifty and a hundred miles in 1940, though. The war saw the end of her marriage to Freddie Dovey, and after it she married George Fleming, a famous record-breaking cyclist and the first man in the UK to ride a twenty-five-mile time trial in less than one hour.

Billie Fleming, as she is remembered now, wanted to inspire women to exercise at a time when many – mostly men it has to be said – considered it wasn't the 'done thing' for women. She wanted to share the health benefits that gave her a full life, thousands of experiences and fame. I'm sure she would have been thrilled to see Tylen take her record and especially thrilled that Amanda Coker holds the new year-mileage world record for both sexes.

Tommy Godwin
5 June 1912 – 1975
The man who rode 200 miles every day for 500 consecutive days

Tommy Godwin, early in his cycling career

Thomas Edward Godwin was born in Stoke-on-Trent shortly before the First World War. He took a delivery job as a twelve-year-old schoolboy. Pedalling his heavy delivery bike quickly saw him build a prodigious level of stamina and fitness, and encouraged by some cycling friends he entered a twenty-five-mile time trial. Not on a racing bike, though – young Godwin couldn't afford one of those – he rode his delivery bike. His only effort at making it faster, apart from pedalling hard, was to remove its wicker basket.

Godwin was fourteen and he did the twenty-five miles in a very fast time for the era. He loved it too, and wanted to race more, so he joined the Potteries Cycling Club ('Potteries' is the collective name for the five pottery-producing towns making up the conurbation of Stoke-on-Trent).

Over the next few years Godwin did hundreds of time-trial races, winning many of them, and proved to be good at all distances, from twenty-five miles to twelve hours. In 1938, and possibly inspired by the efforts of Billie Fleming, Godwin began planning an attempt on the world record for how many miles could be ridden in one year. It was called the Year Record at the time, and was held by an Australian, Ossie Nicholson, with 62,657.6 miles ridden in one year.

It was a huge target but, undaunted, the twenty-six-year-old set off into the unknown on his Raleigh Record Ace bike, equipped with a four-speed Sturmey-Archer hub gear system, at 5 a.m. on 1 January 1939. Proof of the distances he rode would come from a sealed, bike-mounted cyclometer similar to that used by Billie Fleming the year before. He also carried blank cards on which people he met could attest to his location, and with that he could confirm how many miles he'd ridden. The cards would back up the mileage total recorded by the cyclometer.

Godwin had support – not just of a small team of people helping him, but equipment and money supplied by Raleigh and Sturmey-Archer, who got thousands of pounds worth of advertising in return for their investment. There was terrific interest in Godwin's ride.

Financial support is a huge boon for somebody riding all day and every day, and cycling became Godwin's job, but the RTTC, the body governing the UK time trials, decreed that Godwin had given up his amateur status for ever. That meant he could not ride their time trials ever again. This was a big blow because Godwin loved racing. Several of his friends appealed against this decision, but the RTTC would not budge.

Godwin wasn't alone in attempting the Year Record in 1939; two other British riders set off on the same day as him, both with the same intention. Edward Swann ended his attempt after a crash approaching the thousand-mile mark, but the other rider, Bernard Bennett, provided stiff opposition. Bennett matched Godwin quite closely until they reached 50,000 miles. They had been assisted by pacemakers until that point, but they agreed to dispense with them so they could fight for the record on equal terms. That's when the indefatigable Godwin drew ahead, by riding at least two hundred miles per day from the late spring onwards, with 361 miles ridden on 21 June 1939, his highest daily mileage total.

Mind-boggling numbers like that, churned out day after day, saw him ride into Trafalgar Square in London on 26 October with

62,658 miles under his belt. He was the new world-record holder, but there was no rest for Godwin. He continued riding through November and December, eventually amassing 75,065 miles and a Year Record that would last for seventy-six years, but the end of 1939 wasn't the end of Tommy Godwin's record breaking.

At the outset of his record ride Godwin said that if he was still in good shape when his year's ride was done, he would continue riding into 1940 in an attempt to set a new record for the time taken to complete 100,000 miles.

The Second World War was underway by then, and the country was living under blackout laws to avoid assisting the German bombers on their night raids. The short days of winter meant Godwin had to dim his lights when riding at night. Masking his bike lights with sticky tape reduced their beam to a narrow slit in order to prevent them being spotted by enemy aircraft, but it was difficult for Godwin to see the roads in front of him. He had a number of falls. It was also a very cold winter, and that also caused more crashes but, battered and bruised, he carried on. Riding day after day in all conditions requires really good health, and Godwin ascribed his to a lifelong vegetarian diet, although it was heavy on dairy. He was also good at treating and maintaining his own body, and so minimised possible harmful effects of high mileages ridden every day.

Cyclists must pay scrupulous attention to the areas of their bodies that contact their bikes – hands, feet and crotch. Gloves and good shoes help support the first two, and cyclists usually ride with chamois leather inserts to protect their skin from saddle pressure. However, for the third, Godwin found he was more comfortable wearing silk underwear.

His arduous journey finally ended on 15 May 1940, when Godwin arrived at the cycle racing track in Paddington Recreation

Ground, north London, and rode the final mile by circling the track to reach 100,000 miles ridden in 500 consecutive days. A new world record and an average of 200 miles per day, every day.

Reg Harris
1 March 1920 – 22 June 1992
The first cyclist to become
a household name

Reg Harris was world champion in
the track sprint discipline four times

Reg Harris was the fastest track sprinter in the world. World champion five times between 1947 and 1954, once as an amateur and four times as a professional rider, his rags-to-riches story captured people's imaginations. Sponsored by Raleigh for most of his career, the Nottingham company advertising slogan 'Reg Rides a Raleigh' sold three million extra bikes for the manufacturer.

Harris was born Reginald Hargreaves in Bury, Lancashire, on 20 March 1920, the illegitimate son of Elsie Hargreaves. Reg became a Harris when his mother married a local engineer and businessman, Joseph Harris. Nothing interested Harris at school, so he left at fourteen with no qualifications but a burning conviction he would be famous at something. That something was revealed when he bought his first bike.

Initially, Harris toured with the Bury section of the Cyclists' Touring Club, but quickly discovered grass-track racing and that he was very quick. He won his first race, a half-mile handicap at the 1935 Bury sports meeting, and that was quickly followed by other victories. Money could be made in grass-track racing in those days; Reg had found his metier.

There were grass-track meetings all over the UK, run as part of village or town festivals and fetes, and supported by local businesses who donated high-value prizes such as canteens of silver cutlery, china tea services and clocks or jewellery. All things that a fifteen-year-old didn't need but could sell for cash at the meetings, or to friends and family back home.

When he was sixteen, Harris swapped from being a trainee mechanic to working during the winter as a labourer in a paper mill. It was an unskilled job but well paid – well enough to allow him to train and race full-time in the summer of 1936. To all intents and purposes he was already a professional cyclist.

Harris continued racing at track meetings all over northern England, sometimes once but often twice a week. He won prizes at every one, and always had buyers back home for the goods. He quickly became known in Bury and the surrounding area as the lad to go to for luxury items on the cheap. People even sent their wedding present lists to him, with instructions to give relatives first refusal on any items listed if he won them.

And Harris loved the winning itself; he loved the fame it brought too, albeit only in the north of England at this point. But soon he discovered there was potential for much more; bigger victories, more money and much more fame. He read about the wider world of track cycling and discovered that professional sprinters earned big money in the velodromes of Europe.

Still sixteen, Harris entered his first hard-track meeting at the velodrome in Fallowfield, Manchester and won every race. The following winter Harris returned to work at the paper mill, then trained and raced full-time. He did the same in 1938, working in the winter and racing full-time in the summer. He beat the reigning British sprint champion, Dennis Horn, in a sprint match at Fallowfield, which brought Harris selection for Great Britain at the 1939 track-cycling world championships in Italy. Unfortunately, Harris had to wait to prove himself on the world stage because the Second World War broke out while he was training at the Velodromo

Vigorelli in Milan, and the championships were cancelled. It would be four years before he raced internationally again.

Harris, still just nineteen, was recalled from Italy to the UK, where he joined the army, becoming a tank driver who saw action in North Africa. In 1943 his tank was hit and immobilised by a German shell. All the crew except Harris immediately jumped out and were shot. Harris waited for darkness and made his escape into the desert, eventually finding a British military hospital from where he was repatriated. He spent the rest of the war in the UK driving military trucks, which allowed him time to train again and he won the 1944 British track sprint title.

After the war things slowly returned to normal. With more track meetings Harris had more chance to shine and, although he was still an amateur, he attracted sponsorship from the bicycle manufacturer Claud Butler, receiving money as well as equipment. This allowed him to focus entirely on cycling and, after giving up his winter labouring job, he won his first world title, the 1947 amateur sprint at the Parc des Princes in Paris.

With the 1948 London Olympics coming up, Harris became one of the favourites to win a gold medal. British Olympic gold medals were nowhere near as common in the 1940s and 1950s as they are now, so any winner would get huge publicity. Raleigh, spotting Harris's advertising potential, offered to pay him far more than Claud Butler if he rode a Raleigh bike in 1948. With money in his pocket Harris indulged his passion for speed in another way, buying a powerful Jaguar Mark IV car, but was involved in a road accident while driving it before the 1948 Olympics, breaking two ribs. A few weeks later he crashed in a race at Fallowfield and fractured his elbow.

Severely hampered by his injuries Harris took two silver medals at the London Games, in the individual and in the tandem sprint events (tandem is no longer an Olympic sport). Disappointing for him personally maybe, but he got the publicity so it didn't harm his earning potential. Raleigh offered him a contract to race as a professional straight after the Games and paid him a basic salary of a thousand pounds in his first year, plus healthy bonuses for setting records and winning national and world titles.

Harris took his first professional world title in 1949, which boosted his salary from Raleigh and saw high demand from track promoters all over the UK and Europe. Harris was paid very well to race in these meetings – with win bonuses, his salary and his prize money, he was said to have earned in excess of twelve thousand pounds a year for most of the 1950s – something in excess of around £300,000 annually in today's money.

The 1950s were a golden era for track sprinting, with Jan Derksen and Arie van Vliet of Holland, Oscar Plattner of Switzerland, Sid Patterson of Australia, and a whole host of speedy Italians competing as professionals at the world championships, the sprint Grand Prix events held in major European cities and in lots of invitation races held during the summer and winter. Harris had to work hard to beat those riders, but he did. He dominated professional sprinting from 1949 until 1955, winning the world title in 1949, 1950, 1951 and 1954, and taking the bronze medal in 1953 and the silver in 1956.

Harris was a very modern sprinter, powerfully built, like track sprinters are today. His muscular development was phenomenal, and it gave him the power to accelerate quickly and the strength to hold his speed. Harris was less tactical than others of that era, but he was so fast and so strong he didn't need to use sleight of hand. He also held many national and world records, which was testament to his speed, but also to his business acumen. Harris was always careful to break records by small margins, because Raleigh paid him a bonus every time he set a new one, even if the old record was his own.

Harris would have been a contender at the top level in track sprinting today, but he also had presence that would have made him a star in any era. In the 1950s he commanded respect for his athletic powers, but his rags-to-riches story as well as his style and charm also appealed to the British press and public. In 1950 the Sports Journalists' Association chose Harris as their sportsman of the year, which – before the BBC Sports Personality of the Year – was the highest accolade in the UK. Harris was runner up in 1949 and 1951 as well.

His glittering race career ended in 1957; many say because the UCI changed the rules of match sprinting at world championship level, bringing in three-man heats and finals. Three sprinters on the track at once suited more tactical riders and offered the opportunity of collusion. Two riders is a purer form of match sprinting and usually sees the fastest win.

It's also true that Harris, having met many successful business people during his time as a bike racer, fancied himself as a captain of British industry. He threw himself into a number of projects, not all of which succeeded, but he kept his love of cycling. Harris trained hard during his racing career, but when it was over he rediscovered the joy of cycle touring in the countryside, the joy he'd first experienced with the Bury CTC as a young teenager. Reg Harris was cycling near his Cheshire home the day he died of a stroke in 1992 at the age of seventy-two.

Chapter Three
Pioneering women

Until quite recently women who wanted to race on bikes were poorly served by the various governing bodies of the sport. It's almost unbelievable now, but women didn't have their own cycling world championships until 1958. Even worse, they didn't get parity with men's events in the Olympic Games cycling programme until 2012. What's more, it took pioneering women to force these and other issues affecting female cyclists. This chapter looks at the lives and careers of some British cycling legends who helped bring about much needed changes.

Eileen Gray
25 April 1920 – 20 May 2015
Advocate for women's cycling and first female president of British cycling

Eileen Gray, pictured at a social occasion, was a great sports administrator

Eileen Gray was born and grew up in Dulwich, South London. She was academically gifted and became a qualified engineer, quickly working her way up to being a quality controller at an engine factory in central London. It shows the respect in which she was held, being a young woman and achieving a top job in a business that was a male domain in those days.

Engineering was a protected occupation, so when the Second World War broke out she continued working. Her grit and determination showed through when her normal commuting rail line was destroyed during the blitz and she started cycling to work and back. It was no mean feat, navigating bomb-damaged roads and night-time blackouts.

But Gray not only carried on regardless, she found she enjoyed cycling and had an aptitude for it. She joined the Apollo Cycling Club, the only organisation near her which admitted women members. UK governing bodies had never banned women from racing, but some clubs wouldn't have women members – a bit like some golf clubs. Women still raced, but it is impossible to say exactly how many, because the majority took part in time trials. The only stipulation for entering a time trial was that the entrant's cycling club was affiliated to the RTTC. There was no requirement to hold a racing licence. Gray campaigned against prejudice for the rest of her life, doing so persuasively rather than aggressively. She believed there was no reason why women couldn't do what men did and slowly and patiently Gray changed minds.

Gray started competing shortly after joining the Apollo club. She went on to be selected to race for a Great Britain team in a Danish race series. But it was as an administrator and advocate that Gray's biggest talents lay, and that is why she is a British cycling legend. She founded the Women's Track Racing Association in 1949, a body that later became the Women's Cycle Racing Association (WCRA) and, steered by Gray, over the next decades became the key administrative organisation for women's cycling in the UK.

One of the first things Gray did in her developmental role was to seek opportunities for British women to race in continental Europe, and in 1955 she secured an invitation to the first ever female Tour de France. She managed the team herself and one of its members, Millie Robinson, won the race.

That victory was big news in Europe and in the UK cycling press. A magazine called *Coureur*, which was the first UK publication to cover European cycling in depth, devoted seventeen pages to the Great Britain team's exploits, and to Robinson's victory.

The WCRA quickly built its membership, and Gray's tireless, highly professional work saw the body, and women's cycling, grab the respectful attention of world cycling's governing body, the Union Cycliste Internationale (UCI). In 1955 Gray successfully lobbied the UCI for official recognition of women's world records. The UCI didn't at that point either have titles that women could compete for in its world championship programme. That was about to change, and Gray changed it.

The UK governing body, the NCU, which was notoriously old-fashioned and reactionary, wouldn't listen when Gray mooted the idea of women's races at the UCI Worlds. But not having her national governing body's support didn't prevent Gray gaining access to the decision-makers of world cycling. Her arguments were powerful, and in 1958 she got much of what she wanted. Not parity with all the men's world titles, but at least some women's races, specifically a track sprint and individual pursuit, and a road race, at that year's UCI world championships, which were held in France. The first road race was won by Elsy Jacobs of Luxembourg, and two years later Beryl Burton won for Great Britain.

With racing for women established in the world championships Gray went after the Olympics, but found it a lot harder to get the International Olympic Committee (IOC) to accept women's cycling in its programme. It also took a lot longer, all Gray encountered at first was a brick wall of misogyny.

The UCI backed Gray, but her request for the inclusion of women's races in the Olympic cycling programme was dismissed out of hand by the then president of the IOC, Lord Killanin. His ludicrous conclusion that, 'There is no evidence that women's cycling is an international sport,' not only flew against facts, it was a total suspension of reason. Gray wasn't asking for a new sport to be added to the Olympic programme, but for women to be allowed to compete in a sport that was already part of that programme. Women were competing together internationally at the UCI world championships and in other UCI races, refusal to see that was ridiculous.

Eileen Gray didn't let anything stop her, carried on campaigning, patiently lobbying, even though the IOC reduced her to tears, and she prevailed. A women's road race was finally included in the 1984 Olympic Games in Los Angeles. More cycling events were added to the Olympic programme for women over the following years, if slowly. It took until 2012 for women cyclists to get Olympic parity in a number of events. Thank goodness Gray was there to see it, as a venerated guest of the London Games. She

Pioneering women

was also an Olympic torch bearer in her home town of Kingston-upon-Thames.

Gray's other major achievement came in 1977 when she was elected in the first ballot by a sound majority as the first woman president of the British Cycling Federation – now called British Cycling and the governing body for cycle racing in the UK. One of her first jobs in the role was to pitch for and organise the world cycling championships in Great Britain. It was 1982, the second time in the modern era that the UCI world championships had been held in Britain. Track racing was held in Leicester on its one-time, open-air velodrome, and the road events were based on Goodwood in Sussex. The championships were a success, but organising them was fraught with difficulty, particularly when promised sponsorship didn't materialise. People involved say that Eileen Gray shed tears of frustration at times, but she saw the project through, and shed tears of joy at the end.

It was a very emotional moment when Gray stood next to the new British world champion, Mandy Jones, after the medal ceremony. Jones won the women's road race at Goodwood with an impressive performance, one that gladdened the hearts of UK cycling fans. It was a wonderful day.

Eileen Gray's BCF presidency ended in 1985, but she could look back at her legacy with pride. She fought for women to have the same opportunities to race as men did; a simple wish and obvious that it should be so, but it was a long, hard battle. Former president of British Cycling and the first ever British president of the UCI, Brian Cookson, really admired Gray. 'She was skilled at sports governance, skilled in handling people and, although her great contribution was to give women the opportunity to compete, she succeeded not by being radical, but by being logical, patient and very durable. I was a bit in awe of her, to be honest,' he says.

Eileen Gray was awarded an OBE in 1978 and a CBE in 1997, but her true reward for a lifetime of service was to see women cyclists gain parity with men at the 2012 Olympic Games in London. It was also a time of great British cycling success, which was wonderful for us all, but equal rights to compete was Eileen Gray's life mission, and she helped so much to achieve that.

Eileen Sheridan

18 October 1923 – 12 February 2023
The first female cyclist to capture public imagination in the UK

Eileen Sheridan with her record-breaking BSA bike

Eileen Sheridan, born Eileen Shaw in Coventry, was the best at every sport she took part in at school. She was a natural at everything, so it was no surprise that when she joined the Coventry Cycling Club at the age of fifteen, with no intention of competing, she easily kept up with the others on their club runs.

Many keen club cyclists never raced in those days, instead enjoying the camaraderie of belonging to a club of like-minded people who enjoyed exploring the countryside by bicycle. Of course, others were competitive, and a few dabbled with the sport side of cycling while mixing in other activities. Dabbling was all Eileen intended when she competed in an informal ten-mile time trial with members of her club, but her speed impressed everyone. It was 1944, but although other competitive club members encouraged her to race again that year, Eileen didn't compete until the following year, and she started winning.

She quickly became a huge success, setting national records for thirty miles in 1948, fifty miles and twelve hours in 1949 and a hundred miles in 1950. She was also British champion at the fifty and one-hundred-mile distances that year, but she was best at longer distance time trials. Her 1949 twelve-hour British record was set on a day when only four men rode further in the same event. The winner, Des Robinson, who rode for the Great Britain team at the

1952 Helsinki Olympics, only beat Sheridan's distance by six miles. She married Ken Sheridan in 1946 and went on to be British Best All-Rounder competition winner in 1949 and 1950.

Her victories in national championships, the way she rewrote the women's record book and, in particular, how close she got to beating the best men, attracted the attention of the Hercules Cycle and Motor Company. It was one of the biggest sports bike manufacturers in the country and had a flair for marketing. Hercules offered her a lucrative professional contract to attack road records, especially place-to-place road records, riding a Hercules bike and with their name on her racing kit.

As ever, the longer the record distance, the greater the margin by which Sheridan beat previous holders. Five of her records have yet to be beaten, and her thousand-mile record of three days and an hour took forty-eight years to better. (When it was, it was by another formidable long-distance cyclist, Lynne Taylor.)

Her 1954 Land's End to John O'Groats time, set in nowhere near perfect conditions, beat the previous record by eleven hours. Then, after taking a two-hour break at the end, Sheridan carried on to set her phenomenal thousand-mile record.

But Sheridan's story isn't just one of outstanding athletic performances; her tiny frame – she was only 4 feet 11 inches tall – her ever-smiling nature and the sheer health and wellbeing she radiated made her a popular figure during the 1950s. In 1952, she featured in a documentary film called *Spinning Wheels: Cycle Sport '50s Style*. She also featured in a number of national advertisements.

That's how she became the first female cyclist to capture the imagination and the hearts of the British public. It's also why she attracted sponsorship from the Hercules bicycle company, with one of her Hercules bikes on display in the National Cycle Museum today in Llandrindod Wells.

Millie Robinson
3 December 1924 – 23 January 1994
The first British Tour de France winner

Mille Robinson (right)
with Beryl Burton

Jessie Mildred Robinson was born in Ireland, grew up in the Isle of Man, and scored her greatest cycling victories after moving to England. She was the best female British cyclist of her generation and, between 1955 and 1958, the best in the world. She was also the first British winner of a Tour de France.

It was the first ever women's Tour de France actually – the race only survived one year because its existence was complicated by politics and male indifference, but let's talk about Millie Robinson first. She was born in County Mayo into a large farming family, who moved to the Isle of Man in 1949. Millie started cycling while living on the island. She was soon the local champion, but was ambitious and knew she'd have to move to England to progress in her sport.

She did that in 1954, moving to Leeds where she worked for her brother's haulage company, winning her first British national title the following year. She also started competing in road races and dominated most of the few events that were organised for women in 1955. When Eileen Gray, the woman who worked for many years to develop women's bike racing in the UK, heard about the women's Tour de France, Millie Robinson was an automatic selection for the British team.

Eileen Gray's equivalent in France was a man, Jean Leulliot. He could see no reason why women shouldn't have their own Tour de

France. Part of his motivation was political. Leulliot was a communist and Jacques Goddet, who ran the men's Tour, was a staunch conservative. The two men had clashed during the German occupation of France, and their antipathy continued long afterwards.

Leulliot knew that Goddet and the newspaper that owned the men's Tour, *L'Équipe*, would never organise a women's tour, so he decided to do it. His race was called *La Grande Boucle Féminine Internationale*. One meaning of '*boucle*' is loop, and the Tour de France is often called *La Grande Boucle*, meaning The Big Loop. So to avoid copyright conflicts with *L'Équipe*, he knew they would never let him call his race a Tour de France, Leulliot used Grande Boucle Féminine.

But although Leulliot's long-term ambition was to develop his race into a Tour de France for women, the first *Grande Boucle Féminine Internationale* toured just one area of the country – Normandy – and was dominated by the Great Britain team. June Thackeray won stage two and France's Lily Herse led overall until Millie Robinson won stage four on her own. That put her in the race lead with a twenty-five-kilometre time trial and a short road stage to go. Robinson was a great time triallist and forged her overall victory on that time trial stage. It was a pretty dominant victory in a field that was full of talent. Lily Herse, for example, was French road race champion nine times. Robinson would have benefitted from more international competition, but there was very little for women in the 1950s.

One of her greatest international achievements came in 1958 when she set a new world hour record at the Velodromo Vigorelli in Milan. She absolutely hammered the old record, setting new times for ten and twenty kilometres during her attempt. It was an incredible ride, but Robinson was about to be eclipsed by another British woman, Beryl Burton (see next chapter). Robinson will

◌ Pioneering women

always be the first British woman to set a new world hour record, though, and she will always have been the first British cyclist to win a Tour de France. It doesn't matter that it wasn't called the Tour de France – the equivalent race today has only just been named the Tour de France Femmes – it was the spirit of what Jean Leulliot intended for his race in 1955 that counts. That race didn't become what he wanted it to be only because of the indifference of men in charge of cycling in those days.

Chapter Four
Breaking New Ground

Sport's barriers mostly concern performance – completing a certain distance within a certain time, for example. However, British road racing's development from the end of the nineteenth century in itself created a barrier with road racing in Europe. British cyclists didn't take part in the big European road races and didn't perform very well when they did. Some of the British legends in this chapter helped change that. There is also one who broke a magical time barrier and last – but nowhere near least – is a woman who, for many years, was the best in the world and is one of the most outstanding sportswomen of all time.

Ian Steel

28 December 1928 – 20 October 2015
The first British winner of the Peace Race

The Great Britain team at the start of the 1952 Peace Race

Before discussing Ian Steel's life I should explain what the Peace Race was, and why it was so significant. In the aftermath of the Second World War, Europe became divided between western Europe states, with its various democratic forms of government, while the countries of the east were run by communist regimes. The dividing line had been dubbed the 'Iron Curtain' by Churchill, and to cyclists living behind the Iron Curtain under communism the Peace Race was their biggest road event, their Tour de France.

It was a stage race running through the countries of East Germany, Poland and Czechoslovakia. It initially followed a route between capital cities and was called Berlin–Warsaw–Prague, but governments of the communist bloc wanted to promote the idea that communism brought peace to the east, so its name changed to the Peace Race. The overall leader's jersey was yellow with a white dove of peace.

It was the one race every east European cyclist wanted to win. They weren't allowed to take part in the big professional races of the west because communist countries didn't allow their athletes to become professionals. Consequently, eastern European riders often won international amateur races, because they were mature and state-sponsored and cycling was their job. They weren't amateurs in their early twenties aspiring to become professionals, but if they weren't officially professional – they were usually down as serving in the armed services but they served with sports regiments that did very little in the military line – they were full-timers in all but name.

With its tough route and talented, highly trained and highly motivated eastern European competitors, the Peace Race was very hard for western amateurs. It also attracted massive crowds and overall could be an overwhelming and often brutal experience. That is why Ian Steel's win in the 1952 Peace Race was so remarkable, and why he is included in this book. It was a legendary victory.

Steel was born in Glasgow, where his parents ran a shop. He was evacuated west with his sister to the small town of Dunoon at the start of the Second World War. The Steel siblings lived with their grandparents throughout the war, and a few months after returning to Glasgow in 1946, Steel joined the Glasgow United Cycling Club.

He started racing at eighteen and was third in his first race, a twenty-five-mile time trial. It didn't take long for Steel to start winning, and with a string of victories in time trials to his name, he began looking for another challenge. He wanted to try bunched road racing, then banned by the sport's governing body, the NCU. Glasgow Wheelers was part of Percy Stallard's breakaway BLRC organisation so he joined them in 1951 and was soon making a name in road-race bunches.

The BLRC sent teams abroad to race and, representing Scotland, Steel finished second in the Paris–Lens race. That got him a place in the BLRC semi-professional team sponsored by bike manufacturer Viking. Steel won three stages and the overall classification of the 1951 Tour of Britain.

That great debut into road racing brought Steel selection for the BLRC's Great Britain team for the 1952 Peace Race – what a baptism of fire that was. The state of the roads in the post-war east was terrible, but that didn't curb the aggressive racing of riders from the communist countries. The stages were long and the race lasted almost two weeks over a total of 1,326 miles, but the overall average speed was nearly twenty-four miles per hour.

The Peace Race was very political and the start in Warsaw's national stadium was attended by 100,000 people. The guest of honour was high-ranking Russian general Konstantin Rokossovsky, there to demonstrate the Russian influence over the eastern bloc countries. It was so great that many referred to the east as the 'Soviet Bloc'.

Steel took the lead on stage eight to Chemnitz, East Germany, after some impressive mountain riding. After that, Steel came under attack from all the east European teams, who were all under political pressure to win. However, the British riders defended Steel's lead to such good effect that Great Britain ran out the overall team winners. With that, and with Steel's individual victory, team members received prize goodies such as watches and cameras.

Steel's victory was big news in cycling, and even bigger news in eastern Europe, but not much appeared in the mainstream media of the UK, due to an embargo on news from behind the Iron Curtain. The British government did not want to give communism the oxygen of publicity. In Europe, by contrast, and possibly because cycling was so popular there and their amateur riders regularly took part in the Peace Race, Steel's victory was big news. It also made a very big impression on the sport's world governing body, the UCI, which did a lot of good for British cycling.

The UCI was already tired of the war going on between the NCU and the BLRC, with all the petty rules. They threatened the NCU with expulsion if it didn't negotiate peace with the

BLRC. Having two governing bodies in one country looking after different aspects of what was essentially the same sport was ludicrous. The threat worked: the NCU and BLRC began talking and, seven years after Steel's historic Peace Race victory, peace broke out in British cycling with the formation of one governing body, the British Cycling Federation (BCF) which today is simply called British Cycling (BC). This was due in no small part to the performance of Ian Steel.

Brian Robinson

3 November 1930 – 25 October 2022
First British cyclist to win a stage in the Tour de France

Brian Robinson (in sunglasses) racing on the Isle of Man in 1959

Brian Robinson is the godfather of British performance in the men's Tour de France and the other great road races of Europe that are the touchstones of every cyclist's year. Brian was the first; the first British cyclist to finish the Tour de France, the first to win a stage (he eventually won two), and the first to score a top three in one of the five special single-day races called the 'Monuments', with a third place in Milan-San Remo. Jean Bobet, a French former pro who became a great journalist and writer, says that Brian Robinson came to France as a stranger in February 1955, but by May he was part of the pro peloton. He was '*Le premier Anglais*'.

Three years later it was Bobet who spoke up for Robinson after the 1958 Tour de France stage that finished in Brest. Brian had sprinted for victory with an Italian, Arrigo Padovan, and Padovan got ahead and deliberately blocked him. The Italian edged Robinson across the road and towards the crowd barriers, first on one side, then the other. Robinson was obviously stronger, but he couldn't get past. He crossed the finish line in second place, but he thought there was no way the race judges would decide against an established European, so he didn't protest. Padovan was declared the winner.

Later that evening there was knock on Brian's hotel bedroom door. It was Jean Bobet and he was holding the bouquet of flowers they gave to Tour de France stage winners in those days. Bobet handed them to Robinson, telling him the result had been reversed and the stage was his. Jean Bobet had protested on Brian's behalf, and the judges were swayed.

It was the first Tour de France stage a British cyclist had ever won and the French papers were full of it. At a time when cycling didn't feature much in British mainstream sports reporting, there was even half a page in the *Daily Express*. But Brian Robinson wasn't in France for fame and glory – he was an adventurer who felt a pull to be there. He had no roadmap, no mentors, just the desire he discovered as a teenager to race in Europe. As a youngster he had seen beautiful sepia photos of the world's greatest cyclists in magazines his older brother, Des, had brought back from a training camp in France.

Brian and Des Robinson were both cyclists, both talented; both Olympians at the 1952 Helsinki Games. The Olympics were for amateurs back then and Brian Robinson wanted to be a professional in Europe and ride the big road races he read about in his brother's magazines. His chance came in 1955 when the British pro cycling team sponsored by the bike manufacturer Hercules took on a European programme to help get an all-British team into the Tour de France. It would be the first time – Charlie Holland (see chapter two) and Bill Burl had both started the 1937 Tour, but as part of a three-man team with a Canadian, so technically not a British team.

The Hercules team moved as a group to the south of France in February, where the company rented accommodation for the riders and staff, which many of Brian's teammates didn't like. Brian loved it; learning a different French phrase every day, he was soon chatting to his French rivals and discovering other European countries as the racing season progressed. 'To make a success of it you had to live as a Frenchman would, eat French food and adapt to their way of life. It was no good, like many of my teammates did, thinking about what they were missing back home,' he once told me.

His approach worked. Of the British Hercules riders based in France, Robinson was the only one who got results and almost singlehandedly qualified the British team for the Tour. Ten British riders started the 1955 Tour, but only two made it to the finish: Tony Hoar and Brian Robinson. But where Tony was a gallant last, Brian was twenty-ninth overall. He was no plucky trier struggling to get through. Brian Robinson was a player.

Most of the British riders went home after that Tour, but Brian stayed. He had nowhere to live and he didn't have a team, but getting around Europe with a map, a train timetable, living out of a rucksack and staying in hotels or wherever they would have him, he raced for the rest of 1955, paying his way with any prize money he could get.

It was worth it. The following year, after ducking and diving around Europe for a few months, taking opportunities where they were presented, Robinson became the first British cyclist to secure a place in a big French pro team. It wasn't easy, but then I remember sitting next to him at a cycling dinner once and the MC was going round the room interviewing different guests. When he got to Brian he said, 'It must have been so difficult for you in those days, doing what you did.' And I'll never forget Brian's reply: 'People say that a lot to me, but it wasn't difficult really. I was getting paid for what I'd have done for free, it always seemed to be warm and sunny, if you could avoid racing in Belgium; it was an adventure.'

It was, and the next page in that adventure was Brian's second Tour de France stage win, which came in 1959 after a long and well-planned, brilliantly executed lone breakaway. In 1961 he won the big French stage race, the Dauphiné Libéré; his last big victory. Robinson felt he'd gone as far as he could in cycling, and still being young, he wanted to return to Yorkshire and his family, and his career as a builder.

He was successful in his second career too, but rarely spoke about his ground-breaking time as a professional cyclist in Europe.

That changed in 2014 when the Tour de France came to Yorkshire and Robinson was made its patron. Every TV channel, magazine and newspaper in Europe wanted to know about the pioneering Yorkshireman. It was fitting recognition, finally, and lovely to see.

Ray Booty

3 September 1932 – 25 August 2012
The first to break the four-hour
barrier in a 100-mile time trial

Ray Booty in 1956 on his way to beating the four-hour record

In 1954 Roger Bannister broke the four-minute mile barrier in athletics, but there was also a cycling time barrier in the 1950s and it had a four in it. In cycling, one hour for twenty-five miles and two hours for fifty miles had long-since been broken, but two years after Bannister's ground-breaking record, no British cyclist had gone under four hours for a hundred-mile time trial. The sub-four-hour 100 held the same magic in cycling as the four-minute mile had in athletics.

But 1956 was the year it would be broken – by a tall, slim, studious-looking electrician from Nottingham called Ray Booty. Booty was one of the best time triallists and road racers in the UK at the time and was particularly good at longer distance time trials. He was national one-hundred-mile time trial champion from 1955 to 1959, and twelve-hour champion from 1954 to 1958. He also won the British Best All-Rounder (BBAR) competition for the highest average speed in time trials of fifty, one hundred miles and and twelve hours for three consecutive years.

Booty was born in Nottingham, and apart from when he did national service lived in or around that city all his life. His national service – his 'call-up', as they used to say – was done after the war ended, so Booty was able to continue his passion for long-distance cycling, and for racing, while serving in the army. There was a lot of inter-service rivalry in all sports in those days, and Booty became a mainstay of the army cycling team, which competed nationally and internationally.

After the war, Booty worked for Ericsson Telephones in the Nottingham suburb of Beeston, becoming part of the company's cycling club – the Ericsson Wheelers – during his best racing years. He excelled at all long-distance time trials, but his favourite and his best distance was the hundred miles. By 1956 Booty had lowered the British record to 4 hours 1 minute 52 seconds, which he did while winning that year's national championships at the distance.

The next big one-hundred-mile time trial after the championships was the Bath Road 100, held every August bank holiday on an out-and-back course starting just west of Reading. It had a reputation for being a fast course, a place where records were broken. With Booty down to ride the race, having been so close to four hours the month before, thousands of club cyclists rode out to see if he could break the record on the Bath Road. In typical British club racer style of the time, Booty also rode from Nottingham to Reading the day before the race, a one-hundred-mile warm-up for his hundred-mile effort next day.

Race day dawned dry and quiet, almost no wind, ideal conditions for an out-and-back race route. Booty used a single fixed-gear ratio, preferring to pedal smoothly, the ratio defined in accordance with the British standard of measuring such metrics as 84 inches. Let me explain what that means. When Booty raced gear ratios were expressed, at least in the UK, as equivalents to the diameter of a penny-farthing front wheel (the big wheel). Because they were driven directly by the pedals – no chain and gearing – larger diameter penny-farthing wheels travelled further in one pedal revolution than smaller ones. When chain-driven bikes were invented, which gave bikes gearing, the gear ratio was expressed as the equivalent to penny-farthing wheel diameter, so the higher the number in inches (the greater the diameter of the equivalent penny-farthing front wheel) the further the chain-driven bike travelled in one pedal revolution. In Europe gear ratios were expressed as the distance the bike covered during one pedal revolution. Both systems were unnecessarily complicated, and modern cyclists express gear ratios sizes by stating the number of teeth on the chainring and the number of teeth on the sprocket. The equivalent of Booty's 84-inch gear ratio for the 1956 Bath Road 100 would be (approximately) 50 x 16.

What was much more important was to ensure that Booty's gear choice was perfect for the distance, his pedalling style and for the weather conditions that day. He powered his Raleigh Record Ace – a bike he helped make a very popular model – smoothly and cleanly, crouching low and maintaining the same, high-revving pedal cadence over the entire distance. He eventually passed the finish line timekeeper, who stopped his watch at 3 hours 58 minutes 28 seconds. The four-hour barrier for one hundred miles was broken.

Booty carried on winning long-distance time trials and was the Commonwealth Games road race champion in 1958. Then he set an incredible one-hundred-mile solo road record, which – unlike time trials – could be done on straight courses, so it was possible to benefit from a tailwind for the whole distance. His record time was 3 hours and 28 minutes, and it took thirty-four years for anyone to better that. That record underlines just how good Ray Booty was, but he will always be remembered as the man who broke the four-hour barrier for one hundred miles.

Vin Denson

Born 24 November 1935
The first British cyclist to win a stage in the Giro d'Italia

Vin Denson in 1966, dismounting at his historic Giro d'Italia

Vin Denson was born in Chester. Naturally strong, he quickly gained national and international recognition as an amateur rider, then moved to France where that strength saw him gain a place in a professional team. It was a small team at first, but he soon progressed to larger ones. Yet look at Denson's pro cycling career – he only ever won nine pro races.

They were good wins, including one Grand Tour stage, but the real reason Denson progressed in professional cycling was because he understood the role of being a team rider in the sense of being a rider who supports a team leader. Individuals win pro races, but teamwork gets them into the position to win.

Few top riders win consistently without a strong team. *Domestiques*, as they are called in French, serve in many ways. These include pacing the star rider back to the peloton after a stop to fix mechanical problems, or collecting food and extra drinks and delivering them to other team members, or sheltering star riders in crosswinds so they conserve energy.

Denson was good at all of this. In 1963 his work for the Pelforth-Sauvage-Lejeune team was noticed by the best single-day race rider of his generation, the Belgian Rik Van Looy. In 1964 Denson raced for Van Looy's Solo-Superia team to such a good effect that the first five-time winner of the Tour de France, Jacques Anquetil, invited him to join his team, Ford France.

Vin Denson was in the big league now; signing a two-year contract with Anquetil's team for 1965 and 1966 was a real achievement and it opened doors Denson never expected during his cycling career. For example, on the eve of the 1966 Giro d'Italia, which started in Monaco, the whole Ford-France team were invited to Prince Rainier's palace, where the team's riders were presented to the prince and his American wife Princess Grace, the film star Grace Kelly.

Anquetil had won his five Tours de France by 1966. He'd also won the Giro d'Italia twice, the first non-Italian to do so. The Giro wasn't as big a race internationally in the 1960s as it is today, and certainly not as big as the Tour de France, but most Italian team sponsors were interested in the Italian market, rather than a Europe-wide one, so the Giro d'Italia was a crucial shop window.

It might have been more insular than today, but Italian cycling wasn't lacking talent, and that talent was supported by fanatical fans called the *Tifosi*. They didn't think twice about getting involved in a race, pushing their favourites up climbs and booing or even threatening their rivals. During his first attempt to win the Giro d'Italia in 1959, Anquetil was so alarmed at the pushes the spectators gave Italian riders he said, 'If the *Tifosi* could get away with it they would put the Italian riders in their cars and drive them to the top of every mountain climb.'

During the 1966 Giro, Vin Denson felt the rough and rather messy edge of the *Tifosi*'s partisanship. I'll let him tell the story.

'Julio Jimenez, a Spanish rider in our Ford-France team, took the race leader's pink jersey on stage two. He still had it on stage eight, which finished in Napoli, but during that stage Gianni Motta, who was one of the golden boys of Italian cycling back then, got in a breakaway move that went twenty kilometres from the end of the stage. The Ford-France riders started working to catch the breakaway with Motta in it, and we got it down to a twenty-second lead as we entered Napoli, but the *Tifosi* were already booing and shouting abuse at us.

'I was at the front peloton riding hard when we went through some tiny back streets around the docks. One road was about two metres wide, and all the crowd had climbed over the barriers, leaving about half a metre for us to ride on. It was frightening. Italian supporters were screaming at me and threatening me and above us there was all these Romeo and Juliet balconies, about four stories of them, and people up there began emptying their rubbish bins on me. I couldn't get out of the way, so I did a kilometre down this street, and there was spaghetti, tomato juice, beans and everything raining down on me. We saved the lead for Jimenez, though, so I did my job and the team was happy.'

Denson also remembers arriving at the team's hotel after that stage. 'It was a posh place, and you should have seen their faces when I walked in covered in rotting food. But I felt good, pretty fit, so that that evening I told the team manager, Raphael Geminiani that I thought the climbs next day looked like the Pennines in Yorkshire. I could manage the hill in the Pennines, so I asked if I could try to win the stage.

'Geminiani didn't say much, dinner had started and we had some lovely pasta, so I said to Geminiani that if he got me another plate of cappelletti I'd win the stage next day. So he got the extra pasta, and I did win. When the newspaper, *Gazetta dello Sport*, found out about the extra pasta the headline next day read DENSON'S DRUG IS A PLATE OF RAVIOLI.'

It was a good win too, a historic one for British cycling. Denson really went for it; freed from team duties for a day – it wasn't a big mountainous stage, just a hilly one – he raced for himself for once and executed his plan brilliantly, winning the stage alone. It was twenty-one years before another British rider, Robert Millar, won a Giro d'Italia stage.

Denson continued racing as a professional for a couple more years, but says he was very badly affected by the death of Tom Simpson, who died while cycling in the Tour de France in 1967 (see later in this chapter). Not long after that Denson stopped racing and returned to the UK. He started another career in the building trade and went back to his cycling roots, enjoying club rides and taking part in time trials now and again.

Beryl Burton
12 May 1937 – 5 May 1996
One of the all-time greats in any sport

Beryl Burton cycles past Reg Harris with megaphone

This British cycling legend is one of the all-time greats of sport, not just cycling. Beryl Burton reigned supreme on two wheels in Britain from the 1950s until the 1980s, while she was number one in the world from 1959 to 1969, eleven years of world dominance. She was nothing short of a phenomenon. During the second half of the 1960s, Beryl Burton was the equal of any British male rider in the longest distance UK time trials and better than most.

She even broke the British record for the twelve-hour time trial, but wasn't allowed to hold it because it was worded as a 'men's record' and couldn't be held by a woman, even if she had ridden further than all the men. To add insult to injury there was no official woman's record back then, which just underlines how ludicrous cycle racing rules were and how women were held back.

Beryl Charnock was born in Leeds, but grew up in nearby Morley and lived there for the most of her life. Beryl had rheumatic fever as a child, spending many months in hospital, often alone. When she eventually recovered she was warned against doing any form of physical exercise, but her determination knew no bounds. She knew what was best for her, despite what the doctors said, and she achieved some amazing feats of speed and endurance despite having a heart arrhythmia all her life.

Beryl was introduced to cycling in 1953 by her husband Charlie Burton. She joined his cycling club, the Morley CC in West Yorkshire. 'She was handy from the start, but not that competent on a bike,' Charlie once told me. 'We had to push her on club runs sometimes, guide her a bit, but slowly she got better. By her second year of riding she could keep up with any of us, and by the third year she was going out in front and leading us all. I dabbled a bit at time trialling back then, so in 1956 Beryl decided to have a go. She was an instant success.'

Beryl Burton won her first national title the following year in the hundred-mile time trial. With such prodigious talent, Charlie saw the possibility of his wife getting to the very top of the sport, stopped racing and the couple became a two-person team. Beryl competed, and Charlie saw to everything else connected with her racing. In 1959 they travelled to Amsterdam for the world championships and Beryl won her first world title in the track pursuit.

At just three thousand metres, however, the women's individual pursuit wasn't ideal for a cyclist who performed much better the longer a race went. Not that there were any long-distance international races for women: even the road race world championships were around sixty to seventy kilometres (they are much longer now).

In 1960, the amateur world championships were held behind the Iron Curtain in Leipzig, East Germany. Travelling to eastern Europe was difficult in those days and UK cycling's governing body, the British Cycling Federation (BCF), had little experience or money to help. The Burtons weren't put off, and after a few adventures along the way Beryl won the road race and track pursuit world titles in East Germany. She would win the pursuit title three more times; in 1962, 1963 and 1966, taking silver medals in 1961, 1964 and 1968 as well as four bronze medals between 1967 and 1973.

Burton's career continued through the 1960s, becoming even more remarkable as it progressed. By 1967 she wasn't just the best women's racer in the world, she was a class above anyone else. Her only vulnerability was in shorter distances, and at the 1967 world championships in the Netherlands she was beaten on the track by Lyubov Zadorozhnaya in the final of the world pursuit championships. A few days later, Burton proved far too strong for her Russian rival in the road race. Attacking from the start, then riding faster and faster until only Zadorozhnaya could follow her, Burton continued upping the pace until the Russian had to let go. Once alone Burton stretched her lead to 1 minute 47 seconds from Zadorozhnaya by the end of the race – and the Russian was five minutes ahead of the third-placed rider.

Burton was the best, so good that women's racing at that time was too small for her. There were far fewer races for women than there are now, and those that existed weren't demanding enough for her talent. How she would have relished women's road races today, which take place over similar routes to the men's races, although still have slightly shorter distance.

Burton's more remarkable achievements came against male opposition in British time trials. Her crowning glory in that arena was her 1967 twelve-hour record. She beat the male rider who rode the furthest in twelve hours that day, Mike McNamara, both riders beating the existing British record, but McNamara's distance became the twelve-hour record, not Burton's. Beating the best male was one thing, but Burton also beat advances in technology that took place over the next fifty years. Her unofficial women's best performance over twelve hours wasn't surpassed until 2017, when Alice Lethbridge benefitted from some massive aerodynamic advantages.

Burton would have been a huge star today. The longer distances of races like the women's Tour de France, Paris–Roubaix and the other Classics and stage races of the UCI World Tour, would really suit her strength and talent. Her 1967 twelve-hour record is a rare performance in any sport. Women have won world-class, ultra-endurance running races ahead of the best men, but they are races that go on for days. It doesn't usually happen in a discipline that requires strength and speed, as well as endurance.

Beryl Burton was a racer and a cyclist. Cycling wasn't just her sport, it was her transport, her way of seeing the world. The Burtons – Charlie, Beryl and their daughter Denise, who also became a champion – had epic and very adventurous cycling holidays, carrying all they needed on their bikes, often travelling with other members of the Morley Cycling Club. In fact, Beryl was delivering invitations to her fifty-ninth birthday party by bike on the day she died, suffering a heart attack. She was a cycling legend in so many ways, and always will be.

Burton was an incredible person and athlete, a force of nature who recognised no limit and had a huge work ethic. As well as her role in the Burton family, Beryl had a full-time manual job for most of her racing career, working on a farm owned by her friend Nim Carline – another multi-national champion from Morley. She has been much missed by Yorkshire and by British cycling, a legend in her lifetime and a British cycling hero.

Tom Simpson

30 November 1937 – 13 July 1967
The first British cyclist to reach the pinnacle of men's professional road racing.

Tom Simpson rides a lap of honour at the Parc des Princes in Paris after finishing sixth overall in the 1962 Tour de France

If Brian Robinson opened the doors of men's world-class road racing for British cyclists, Tom Simpson blew those doors off their hinges. Some experts, including Britain's first-ever Tour de France winner Sir Bradley Wiggins, as well as many cycling fans, say that Tom Simpson is the still best all-round male road racer the UK has ever produced, despite all the UK cycling success of recent years. It's an opinion that stands scrutiny.

Simpson has the best record by far of any British male in single-day races, in particular the biggest Classics. He was the first British rider ever to win one of the five Classics known as the Monuments. Mark Cavendish is the only other British man to have won a Monument, but where Cavendish won only one, Tom Simpson won three. Simpson was also the first British men's elite road race world champion. Again, only Mark Cavendish has equalled that.

The manner of Simpson's single-day race victories was astonishing too. For example, he won the Tour of Flanders, the pride and glory of this bike-mad region of Belgium, at his first attempt and at the age of twenty-three. It's a tenet of men's pro cycling that the Tour of Flanders requires experience or huge local knowledge for success, Simpson had neither. Not only did he win the Tour of Flanders in 1961, he took fifth place the following year and was third in 1963. Those results are still the three best British men's placings in this race. Barry Hoban in 1967 and Luke Rowe of Team Sky (now known as INEOS Grenadiers) in 2016 are the only two British riders to come anywhere near Simpson in Flanders.

Simpson's other two Monument victories show the range of his talent. In 1964, he won Milan–San Remo – said now to be the sprinter's Monument, also won by Mark Cavendish. In 1965 he won Il Lombardia, which only the best climbers can win. With his cobbled Monument victory in Flanders, that's an impressive range of abilities.

Simpson was also consistent. In 1963, he was placed in the top ten of every classic, which brought him second place to Jacques Anquetil of France – one of the all-time greats – in that year's world rankings. Simpson was also second to Anquetil in 1965.

Simpson's victory in the 1965 professional road race world championships was an incredible achievement. Not only had a British cyclist never won the title before, he had a small, albeit very effective, British team backing him in a race that had been dominated by Europeans since its inception. Simpson's world title was big news in the European media, and it massively increased people's awareness of him in the UK. So much so that in December 1965 he became the first cyclist ever to be voted BBC Sports Personality of the Year, beating icons of British sports like Jim Clarke, Bobby Moore and Henry Cooper.

Simpson was also a very good stage race rider, with several victories in week-long races to his credit. If he had an achilles heel, though, it was in the Tour de France, and that was more due to lack of team support than talent. Simpson was the first British yellow jersey winner in the Tour, taking the lead in 1962 during a Pyrenean mountain stage. He was lying third with three stages to go when he crashed, breaking two fingers, subsequently dropping to sixth when he was unable to pull with any force on his handlebars during the final time trial.

But as his career progressed Simpson became increasingly determined to win the Tour, saying, 'All the true greats of the sport have won that race, and I want to be remembered as a true great.' That drive to win would cost him his life.

Looking back, it's clear that Simpson set himself a near impossible target. Where it is possible to win single-day races – even Monuments – without strong team backing, it's incredibly difficult to do so in the Tour de France. Simpson never had a strong team. The strongest was Gitane-Leroux, who Simpson raced for in 1962. Its manager, Raymond Louviot, believed in Simpson's talent and put that belief above French pride. When Simpson transferred to the Peugeot-BP team in 1963, he never had the same support. His 1964 Tour result was a disappointing fourteenth overall. Then he was injured in crashes in 1965 and 1966 Tours and couldn't finish either. But the common thread in those three Tours was Peugeot-BP racing as a group of individuals, not as a team.

He was still with Peugeot in 1967, but the Tour de France organisers decided to revert to the national team formula for the 1967 race. It was the formula used from 1930 to 1961, and the decision was political rather than practical or economic. Everyone thought it a retrograde step, except Tom Simpson. Now he didn't have to sign for Peugeot-BP for the following year as a condition of the team selection for the Tour, leaving him free to sign a far more lucrative contract to race for the Italian Salvarani team in 1968 and 1969. Although the 1967 Great Britain team wasn't the strongest in the 1967 Tour De France, it would be dedicated to him.

There was a great sense of mission around the British team when the 1967 Tour de France started. Simpson had focused the whole of 1967 on an attempt to win, or at least finish in the first three in the Tour. In March he won the Paris–Nice stage race, ahead of all his Tour de France rivals. He also rode the three-week

Vuelta a España, which was held before the Tour de France, and won two stages.

The 1967 Tour started well, Simpson made two decisive moves in the first week; first on the cobbled stage to Roubaix, then on the mountain stage to the top of the Ballon d'Alsace in the Vosges Mountains. When the race entered the Alps he was lying seventh overall and very much in contention, but then he picked up a stomach virus and lost time on the stage that went over the mighty Col du Galibier. By the end of the stage he was still seventh, but his time deficits had increased.

The situation was the same at the start of stage thirteen, which climbed another iconic Tour de France mountain, Mont Ventoux in Provence. The day was stifling hot, and although Simpson was still unwell he told teammates that he felt better and would attack on the climb.

All looked good for a while; Simpson was able to follow the best climbers on the Ventoux and was in the small leading group at the point where the road emerges from a forest with four miles left to the summit. The full heat of the sun fell on the riders and Simpson began to struggle. He couldn't hold the pace set by the leaders and dropped back to a small but select chasing group. It included the eventual stage winner, Jan Janssen, and Simpson would have been better staying with that group, but he didn't. He kept attacking, trying to break away, and eventually his strength gave out.

Just over a mile from the summit, Simpson began to weave across the road and a few seconds later he collapsed. The Great Britain team mechanic Harry Hall, following in a car behind Simpson, was first to him and he saw the rider wasn't breathing. Hall administered what first aid he knew, the Tour de France doctor was quickly on the scene, but nothing could be done; Tom Simpson was dead.

The conclusion of an autopsy was that he had died of heart failure brought on by heatstroke and dehydration, it was also noted that traces of amphetamine metabolites were found in his body and evidence he had taken amphetamine found in his race jersey pockets. Amphetamine was in regular use in men's professional road racing in those days, but it was against the doping regulations.

Using amphetamines was something Simpson had talked about with close friends and family. He was uncomfortable with it, but said he wasn't going to be beaten because someone else had taken a pill. Judge Tom Simpson as you will, but those are the facts, and he is a British cycling legend.

Chapter Five
Seventies' Flare

The 1970s was a time of transition for British cycling. Early in the decade cycling in the UK was still reeling from the death of Tom Simpson during the 1967 Tour de France and for a while Barry Hoban was the only British cyclist competing at the very top of men's road racing. The decade still had its legends though, and some young British cyclists were trying to make their way in the big European races, especially towards the end of that period.

Barry Hoban
Born 5 February 1940
Britain's first Tour de France multi-stage winner

Barry Hoban at the peak
of his long career in 1974

Barry Hoban is a Yorkshireman from Wakefield. He was a good track, time trial and road racer as an amateur. He was national champion in the individual pursuit and the fifty-mile time trial, then in 1962 he followed the path taken by Tom Simpson, who he'd competed against in the UK, and moved to France to race as an amateur.

Based in Lapugnoy (the far north of France), living in a similar coal mining community to the one he grew up in, Hoban started competing in French amateur races. After a number of successes he took independent status – a sort of halfway house category that existed in the 1960s and into the 1970s between amateur and some professional races. Hoban made his mark, and at the start of 1964 became a fully professional rider with the French Mercier-BP team, earning a surprisingly good income for the time. The team really made him work for it, as he recalls here: 'My contract with Mercier was for twenty-one pounds per week, which was great in those days when Manchester United footballers only got paid twenty pounds a week. On top of that there were bonus payments, and a share of the prize money, so I was making sixty or seventy pounds a week. I had quite a bit of money saved up by the end of that year, but boy did I earn it. I think I raced in everything.

'I rode all of the Classics, then the Vuelta a España. I won two stages in it, so I was the first British rider to win a Vuelta stage. Then

Seventies' Flare

my team manager, Antonin Magne, put me in the 365-miles-in-one-go Bordeaux–Paris, which took a lot of preparation and recovery to do it properly, and I got neither. I wanted to ride the Tour de France, but because I was still going well Magne made me ride the Midi Libre stage race. I ended up tired before the Tour de France started, but I still got through it and nearly won a stage in Bordeaux.

'After it I was knackered, but Magne still put me in all the races right up to Il Lombardia at the end of the season, I didn't finish that one. I rode all the races Magne put me in through to the end of the year, and just got even more tired. I didn't really feel back to full strength until the beginning of 1966.'

In 1967, Hoban was fifth in the Tour of Flanders and came very close to winning a classic later on in the year, when Rik Van Looy beat him by a tyre's width in Paris–Tours. In 1968 Hoban, who later became known as a sprinter and a very good single-day racer, did something he rarely gets credit for. He became the first British cyclist to win a mountain stage of the Tour de France. It was a big one too, in the Alps. Here's Hoban describing that landmark victory:

'There was an intermediate sprints competition in the 1968 Tour, and I needed to score points before the climbers and contenders got going on that stage. There was a sprint in Albertville, before the climbs, so I attacked quite early in the stage to try and win it. Problem was Andrés Gandarias of Spain came with me, and he was lying fifth overall. I knew I wouldn't stay away if he came with me, so I told him I was only going for the sprint points and wouldn't work with him after that.'

Gandarias dropped back to the peloton but, having won the sprint points, Hoban had a good gap on the rest, so he kept going. He climbed the Col des Aravis alone and although some of the good climbers had attacked behind, and Hoban lost some of his lead going uphill, he gained more time over his chasers going down.

He lost some time going up the next big climb, but still had six minutes' lead at the summit. He added to that on the descent and maintained his steady effort along the Arve valley to Sallanches. At the foot of the final climb to the village of Cordon, Hoban still had a good lead and by pedalling his lowest gear at a conservative but a steady pace he won an Alpine stage, right beside Mont Blanc, the highest mountain in France, by four minutes.

There were other British firsts in Hoban's career. In 1969 he became the first British cyclist to win more than one stage in any single Tour de France, as well as the first from his country to win two consecutive stages. Those wins took Hoban's total to four, the first British rider to reach that number during their career. He ended with eight stage victories in the Tour de France and is still second behind Mark Cavendish in the British Tour de France all-time stage win rankings.

He is still the only British cyclist to get a top three placing in climbing and cobbled Monuments, which he achieved with third in the 1969 Liège–Bastogne–Liège and the 1972 Paris–Roubaix. He is the only UK rider to win the Classic Gent–Wevelgem, in 1974.

Barry Hoban had a long and distinguished career, racing for some of the biggest pro teams from 1964 until 1979, often as the only British rider in the world's biggest road races. British cycling seemed to suffer a crisis of confidence after Tom Simpson's death in 1967, but Hoban helped rebuild that confidence and pave the way for others to become British cycling legends during the 1980s and onwards until the present day.

Hugh Porter
Born 27 January 1940
Four-time world champion on the track

Hugh Porter was a powerful road racer as well as a track champion

Wolverhampton-born Hugh Porter was another tall, strong, natural cyclist, very like Graham Webb (see next entry). Good in road races and on the track as an amateur, Porter continued mixing the two disciplines throughout his professional racing career. However, he achieved legendary status on the track with a record-breaking four world titles in the demanding discipline of the individual pursuit for professionals.

As an amateur Porter won a silver medal in the pursuit at the 1967 world championships, but he really came into his own after he turned pro. The amateur pursuit distance was 4,000 metres, but the professional distance was 5,000 metres, and it was as a professional that Porter won his four world titles. This is how he explains why the longer distance suited him: 'I wasn't as explosive as some pursuiters are, which means I wasn't as good as some at accelerating from a standing start. That suits more sprinter types, and I wasn't a sprinter. But once I got going, the longer 5000-metre distance allowed me to get back any time I lost at the start, and to gain more on my opponents.'

Porter also preferred riding pursuits on big, outdoor rather than shorter, indoor tracks, where his slower start made him vulnerable. In pursuit races one rider – or one team – starts on one side of the track and the other starts on the opposite. They then pursue each other, hence the name, but the rules of the event say that if one rider, or team, catches the other, the catcher wins and the caught is eliminated. A talented, explosive rider, who gambled everything on a fast start, could catch Porter on a short indoor track. Ferdi Bracke of Belgium did it in the final of the 1969 professional pursuit world championships, which were held on the 250-metre Antwerp indoor track. Porter won all his world titles on outdoor tracks of at least 333.33-metre circumference.

Porter won his first pro pursuit world title in 1968, on the big outdoor Olympic velodrome in Rome. It was his passport to the lucrative winter six-day season, which was held on indoor velodromes throughout Europe. Six-day races paid the riders taking part very well and had a big following, but they were hard – 'Not as hard maybe as they had been in the past, when one rider from each two-man team had to be on the track for the whole six days, but still hard enough, with long Madison races. Not one-hour Madison races like they have in the six days today, ours were often a hundred kilometres long, and if the big stars were fighting for superiority that is a long time to be racing flat out,' he says.

Porter won three further professional pursuit world titles, in 1970, 1972 and 1973 and by doing so his world champion status ensured he was well paid through each winter six-day season, but Porter kept busy each summer too, winning a number of British professional road races.

In 1968, with the Tour de France running a two-year experiment by going back in time and inviting national and regional teams to the race, instead of trade-sponsored ones, Porter was selected for the Great Britain Tour team. 'The selectors thought I might be able to win the short prologue time trial they used to start Tours with back then, because the 1968 prologue was just a little bit longer than a pro pursuit race. But prologue time trials on street circuits aren't the same as pursuits on the track. All the street corners mean you can't get a constant rhythm going and I finished seventh. It wasn't bad – I mean, up in the top ten in the Tour – but I'd picked up an injury before the race and it flared up again on stage three, so I had to stop,' Porter explains.

Porter began another career in sport once he stopped racing, and he became famous and highly respected all over again. Starting as a sports reporter on local radio, he eventually became a key part of the BBC's national sports commentating team. Porter worked at the biggest races, including many world championships and the Olympic Games, where his insight and descriptive powers helped viewers and listeners understand what was happening in races.

He also formed an incredible partnership with his wife, the Olympic swimming gold medallist, Anita Lonsbrough, as an on-site race commentator team. She ensured Porter always had up-to-date information; totally true professionals and both legends of their sports.

Graham Webb

13 January 1944 – 28 May 2017
The last British cyclist to win the men's amateur road race world title

Graham Webb pictured just after winning the 1967 amateur road race world title in the Netherlands

Graham Webb was born in Birmingham, a natural athlete with huge physical capacity. He also showed that being a professional cyclist was still a very risky career choice in the 1960s and that teams didn't invest in their riders. Things could quickly go wrong and, when they did, there was often no way back.

Webb had an inauspicious start in life. He was the youngest of five children, whose father was killed during the Second World War. His mother struggled and Graham told me one of his abiding memories from those days was never getting enough to eat. His playgrounds were the bombed-out streets. With that start in life it was inevitable his health suffered and during successive bouts of pneumonia he was given the last rites twice. In the end he was saved by a bicycle.

'I built it from bits and pieces salvaged from the rubble on the bomb sites, but as soon as it was serviceable I started riding crazy miles, like a hundred miles from Birmingham to Gloucester and back, trying to do it non-stop. I managed to do it the third time I tried,' he told me.

Since Webb was doing those early long rides, sports scientists have discovered that people respond differently to training, and they respond with a wide range of adaptation to training stimuli. Most of us lie in the middle of the adaptation bell curve, but at either end of that curve a very small number hardly adapt at all to any training, while at the opposite end of the curve are an equally small number of super-adaptors.

Graham Webb must have been a super-adaptor, because his body responded to every one of those long rides, and he quickly got stronger and stronger. At the age of seventeen, with a bike not much better than the one he started on, and certainly worse than the other competitors rode, Webb entered his first race. It was a twenty-five-mile time trial, and he won it, coming very close to a sub-sixty-minute time for the distance.

Not many seventeen-year-olds could ride that fast in those days, and certainly not on a cobbled-together bike. Webb won more time trials, gaining support with better equipment provided by local bike shops. He started road and track racing, soon winning in those disciplines.

It wasn't long before Graham Webb was a national champion and one of the best amateur racers in the country. In search of a bigger challenge, and already thinking he might be able to make a career from cycling, Webb moved to the Netherlands in 1967. Once there he discovered his speed and power was a perfect fit for their road races. There are stories of him lapping the field in Dutch races, run on short urban street circuits, not once but sometimes twice.

While fitting in as many of these races as he could, Webb carried on training over long distances. He was selected to ride for the British team for the 1967 amateur road race world championships, which by coincidence were held in the Dutch city of Heerlen.

Heerlen is in the only hilly region in the Netherlands, in the far south-east of the country, squeezed between Belgium and Germany. The hills there are steep, but relatively short; power climbs, as they are called in cycling, and Webb had buckets full of power. When the winning breakaway formed towards the end, Webb chased and just cruised up to it. He rode right by it and won easily. In his wake he left riders of the calibre of René Pijnen, who later became a very good professional rider, and Roger De Vlaeminck, one of the best professionals in the world, a winner of all five of the Monuments. Graham Webb made them look second rate that day.

Suddenly Webb was the hottest prospect in amateur cycling, and when he became a professional rider that winter with the Mercier-BP team, it's said that his basic salary was higher than the great Eddy Merckx received when he first became a professional in 1965. Merckx was the amateur road race world champion too. Of course, with Webb's great new salary came great new expectations and he ran into problems right at the start of 1968.

He spent January training in Sardinia, but ended up stranded there by a transport strike when the racing season started. He missed the first races in the south of France, and when he finally made it to the French mainland all his bikes and clothing were stolen out of his car during an overnight stop on the long drive to Belgium.

He had to borrow a bike, borrow clothes and shoes to take part in the first big Belgian race of the year, Het Volk (now known as Het Nieuwsblad). Webb had a mechanical problem in that race with his borrowed bike, and didn't finish. Next day in the Kuurne–Brussels–Kuurne race he suffered terrible knee pain. The same thing happened a few days later on the first stage of Paris–Nice, only now the pain was so bad he couldn't continue.

The cause of Webb's knee pain was the cycling shoes he'd borrowed after his were stolen. In the 1960s, cycling shoes were nowhere near as sophisticated, or adaptable, as they are now. Back then each cyclist had to painstakingly set up their shoes. The shoe plates tacked to the soles, which positioned their feet correctly on the pedals, had to be set up by the rider according to their foot shape, size and their individual pedalling style. Riding in someone else's shoes had upset the fine balance of Webb's pedalling, straining his knee tendons and resulting in tendinitis. When tendinitis sinks its fangs in, the main cure is rest.

His team reacted in the short-term way professional cycling teams did in those days. Webb says that Mercier-BP stopped paying him while he was resting. Once his knee was fixed, Webb spent the rest of 1968 mostly based in Belgium, where he rode their professional Kermesse races, a tough school to fight in.

He won four Kermesses, informed his French team of his results, but got no reply. At the end of 1968 his contract was terminated, and Webb was left with no alternative but to join a little-known Belgian team, which quickly ran out of money. Faced with racing just for the money he could win in Kermesses again, Webb got a job in a Belgian furniture factory. He eventually became a crane driver, married a Belgian woman and stayed in that country for the rest of his life.

Over the years he became more Belgian than British, and during an interview I did with him towards the end of his life Webb told me that he even dreamt in Flemish, the language of his Flanders region. At one point he made a comeback to racing, winning four Belgian national track titles racing under the rules of a non-UCI cycling federation in Belgium.

He loved Flanders and enjoyed riding his bike through the flat countryside where he lived near the Dutch border. It was his home and because cycling is so popular there, to many Flemish people Graham Webb was always a '*Wereldkampioen*' ('world champion'), and that really meant something to him.

Les West

Born 11 November 1943
Fourth in the 1970 professional road race world championships

Les West winning a stage of the 1965 Milk Race in the UK

If you aren't familiar with cycling, you might wonder why fourth place in one race is reason for inclusion in a book filled with stories about world champions and Tour de France pioneers. Well, the answer is that it is worthy simply because of what that means: its status in the sport. The professional road race world championships – now called the men's elite road race world championships – is a massive deal in cycling. Only two British men have ever finished higher than Les West did in 1970, and nobody who raced entirely in the UK as a professional has ever come near him.

But the 1970 world championships are not West's full story. He was an incredible bike racer, but the most laidback and unassuming person you could ever meet. Even the most unassuming of the others in this book, Brian Robinson, for example, had a need to achieve, a need to prove himself in cycling by going as far as he could with his ability. West didn't seem to have that; he just liked cycling – he still does when the weather is good. He was a tough competitor in a race, of course he wanted to win, but he felt no need to go as far as he could in the sport. Here's an example.

West won the 1965 and 1967 editions of the Milk Race, the Tour of Britain stage race sponsored by the Milk Marketing Board. And between those two victories West took the silver medal behind Evert Dolman of the Netherlands at the 1966 amateur road race world championships, held on the Nurburgring circuit in Germany. That was big news in continental cycling, where international amateurs raced for sponsored cycling clubs, or those from the communist bloc countries were state sponsored; either way, cycling was their full-time job. That's why European countries and Russia dominated amateur cycling. In contrast, West worked full-time as a telephone engineer and did so throughout his cycling career, even when he was a professional.

West's silver medal was big news, and several European professional teams wanted him to join, including one of the best, the Bic team, which had taken over Jacques Anquetil's Ford-France. But there was a misunderstanding, due mainly to conflicting stories in the European sports press, about which team West would race for in 1967 and the contract from Bic never arrived. Tom Simpson, Barry Hoban or Brian Robinson would have followed up. West, by contrast, thought Bic must have simply changed their mind and let the matter rest. I'm not making a value judgment, just stating a fact.

Instead of turning professional in France, West stayed in the UK and set his sights on doing well at the 1968 Olympic road race in Mexico City. He was a shoe-in for selection and was in great form, but a puncture early on, compounded by a long wait for a service vehicle with a replacement wheel, delayed him. Once he got going, West's bike developed another mechanical problem causing two more stops to fix it. After riding alone for thirty miles, he had to accept the inevitable and quit the race.

With a four-year wait to the next Olympic Games, West decided to turn professional, 'mainly for a change of racing really', he says. By the late 1960s there was a programme of professional road races in the UK and a group of British based riders in British pro teams to ride them. West joined them in 1969, racing for the Holdsworth team. There wasn't much money to be made, which is why West kept his telephone engineer's job. 'The British pro races weren't as long as they were in Europe and, with fewer riders, nowhere near as hard, so I didn't need to do the sort of training they did in Europe. I trained Tuesdays and Thursdays after work, then raced at the weekends throughout my cycling career,' West says.

The British pro racing scene would grow throughout the 1970s, but the decade kicked off with the cycling world championships being held in Britain for the second time in history. The events were based on the city of Leicester, where the track disciplines were held at the old Saffron Lane Velodrome and the road races were based on the Mallory Park motor-racing circuit, where each race started and finished and passed through on each lap.

The men's professional road race was the biggest attraction. There was a star-studded field and the race started fast – too fast for West. 'It was my own fault, I was too far back in the main bunch and with the speed we were doing it was impossible to move up. We did a few laps like that, then on this one long crosswind section the race split. I was in the back half and we quickly lost time on the front riders. I thought that was it, race over, but then we turned a corner and all the front riders were sat up and going slowly.

'All of a sudden, I got a second chance, so I thought, Right, don't make the same mistake again, make the effort and get right to the front ready for when the attacks start again. But just as I got to the front of the bunch I saw a small breakaway was a little bit ahead, so I carried on sprinting and quickly got up to them. It was a good breakaway too, so I thought this might be all right.'

It was all right. Other members of the breakaway included Jean-Pierre Monseré of Belgium, the Dane Leif Mortensen and the Italian Felice Gimondi; all with proven records, all in great form and all listed as pre-race favourites. West held his own with them, working hard and the breakaway stayed clear.

Monseré attacked close to the finish and stayed ahead, winning the world title for Belgium. Mortensen was best in the sprint for second place against Gimondi, who finished third, and West was fourth, unable to sprint because his legs had totally cramped up. The pro road race in the world championships is always in the region of 260 kilometres (162 miles) long. West rarely raced over that distance, while the vast majority of riders in the pro world championships did. Those riders were also full-time, well-paid professionals, they didn't have to mend telephone lines during the day then squeeze their training in after work. And for that reason alone, for achieving the high standard he did, while training the same as most British amateur club racers, Les West is most definitely a British cycling legend.

Alf Engers
Born 1 June 1940
Making time trialling a spectator sport and riding twenty-five miles inside fifty minutes

Alf Engers racing at London's Herne Hill Velodrome during the 1960s

Alf Engers, known to many as King Alf, was the rock-star of 1970s' British time trialling. He was glamour in an essentially private sport; reviled by the authorities, but loved by those who watched and took part. Before Engers the only spectators at British time trials were relations or friends of competitors; when he raced, thousands turned out to watch, lining dual carriageway flyovers and standing wherever they were allowed.

Engers was talented, dedicated, driven and fast. He broke the time trial barrier of his age by riding faster than 30 m.p.h. for twenty-five miles, but there was something more to him. Riders before and after him were talented, dedicated, driven and fast, and they broke time trial barriers, but they had nowhere near the following of Engers. Why was that?

His battles with authority were one reason for his popularity, especially with younger cyclists. Engers was something of a rebel, while the administrators of the RTTC (Road Time Trials Council, the body controlling time trials in the UK) were traditionalists. Engers was no respecter of authority or tradition and at times no respecter of rules, especially if he thought they were petty. That brought him into conflict with the rule makers.

But there was more. Engers would arrive at races in his sponsor Alan Shorter's Jaguar, dressed in a long Afghan coat and wearing a

Seventies' Flare

wide-brimmed felt hat. He occasionally had long hair, his appearance similar to the likes of Jimi Hendrix and other late sixties' and early seventies' rock stars. He was a total contrast to everybody else who took part in time trials.

Alfred Robert Engers was born in north London and started cycling on a bread delivery bike at the age of ten. His school sports were swimming and running, but his performance was compromised when he fell off his bike at fourteen and damaged his kneecap so badly it was removed. By then, though, he had started cycling with the Barnet Cycling Club and began racing.

His rebellious nature got him into trouble shortly after his accident, and he was expelled from school. That allowed him to start work, becoming a baker and pastry cook. He worked nights in the bakery for most of his cycling career, leaving time in the day to train.

Engers made steady progress in time trials until he set a new British record for twenty-five miles of 55 minutes 11 seconds in 1959. He was just nineteen, so was held to have potential and was offered a contract to race as an independent rider – a sort of semi-professional – by a London bike dealer called Ted Gerrard.

The independent category was created for racers to try professional cycling while still being able race with amateurs. It didn't work out for Engers; family and business commitments restricted his opportunities to race, so he applied to the cycling authorities for the return of his amateur status. They refused and continued refusing for the next five years. He'd obviously angered someone in authority, but it was easy to do that. Officials wielded their authority like legal sledgehammers. There were examples of cyclists being suspended from competition, particularly by the RTTC, for quite minor breaches of rules and often for lengthy periods.

Engers was finally granted amateur status in 1966 and gained access to his sport again. He was fully mature, and full of desire.

Over the next ten years he became unbeatable over twenty-five miles, winning the British championships at the distance in 1969, then every year from 1972 to 1976.

The British twenty-five-mile time trial championships is often called the 'blue ribbon' of that section of the sport. It's the time trial distance most cyclists have competed at. It's a distance that suits track racers and pursuiters just as much as it does specialist time triallists, and many good road racers can do a fast twenty-five-mile time. That means it is the most hotly contested British time trial title, but Engers beat all comers, year after year. Soon, though, winning wasn't enough. Engers wanted to be the fastest on record.

The fastest times in British time trial competition are called competition records, and Engers set new competition records for twenty-five miles five times before 1978. The record by then was his – fifty-one minutes exactly. But if a cyclist can ride twenty-five miles in fifty-one minutes the tantalising questions is, can they get below fifty? Sub-fifty for twenty-five miles means riding faster than thirty miles per hour for the distance, which at that time had a special aura in UK cycling.

It would need a perfect day and a perfect bike. In those days that meant a light bike. Engers was famous for having the components of his bikes drilled and pared of any excess metal to reduce their weight. His bikes were designed specifically for time trialling by his friend, mentor and personal sponsor Alan Shorter. Shorter did everything he could to reduce a bike's weight, once cutting slots in the head tube of a frame for Engers, which whistled when he rode it at speed.

Shorter and Engers also had a feel for the effects of aerodynamic drag on cyclists. It was before disc wheels, aerodynamic handlebars and framesets; all they could do was modify and refine the classic race bike design. One of Engers's bikes had its brake levers mounted behind the handlebars to remove them from the air flow. The only way he could operate them when holding the bottom of his dropped handlebars was by pressing them with his forearm, which wasn't safe at all.

Engers also raced with huge gear ratios. The fastest UK time trial courses were flat and took place on dual carriageways, where traffic passing a cyclist assists slightly. Using a high gear ratio takes advantage of that situation, while the slow pedal cadence they dictate means a rider can sit rock solid on their bike, improving their aerodynamics.

Engers developed his own training ideas, using the winter to ride lots of miles and build stamina. In summer he would compete in mid-week track meetings or ten-mile time trials to build his speed.

The perfect day came on the 5 August 1978. Engers was at peak fitness, he had his latest and lightest bike with just three different gear ratios on it. The course he was racing was in Essex, and was a flat dual carriageway and the weather was perfect. British time triallists used to talk about 'float' conditions in which it was possible to ride faster for the same effort. One observation was that these conditions came just after rain, so maybe the reason why it was possible to ride faster was low air pressure.

Air pressure makes a significant difference when cycling at speed. Aerodynamic drag increases exponentially as speed increases arithmetically, so a cyclist accelerating from 29 m.p.h. to just above 30 m.p.h., a one-mile-per-hour increase, has to push more air aside. If air pressure is lower, the air is not so dense and creates less drag, allowing the cyclist to ride faster for the same effort.

The twenty-fifth of August was float day. An earlier starter in the Essex twenty-five-mile time trial, Eddie Adkins, recorded a time of 50 minutes 50 seconds, breaking Engers's record. But Adkins didn't hold the record for long; a few minutes after he crossed the finish line Engers flew over it, recording a time of 49 minutes 24 seconds. It was a new British competition record, and Engers was the first man in the UK to ride faster than thirty miles per hour for twenty-five miles.

Afterwards, he talked about being in a 'state of grace' that day and it was a formidable performance. The record stood until 1990 and was broken by a man riding a low-profile bike with a disc wheel and aerodynamic tri-bars, meaning his bike had much more speed potential than that ridden by Engers. To provide further context, the time trial bikes of today are so aerodynamic it's reckoned that riding a modern bike provides at least a five-minute advantage over a standard road race bike. Remove five minutes from Engers's 1978 time and you get around forty-four minutes for twenty-five miles, ballpark for the competition record today. No wonder King Alf Engers is a British cycling legend.

Sid Barras

Born 3 April 1948
First British cyclist to win and lead the Tour of Switzerland and the king of city centre racing

Sid Barras pictured during a Viking team training camp in Majorca

Sid Barras is from Teesside in north-east England, where he had his earliest cycling experiences and racing success. His love of cycling in the rugged terrain of the nearby north Yorkshire moors saw Barras develop quickly. He was strong and fast from an early age, so he could win in all sorts of terrain.

He became a professional cyclist in 1970 for the British-based team Bantel, and just carried on winning. Barras won 380 races during his eighteen-year professional cycling career, many of those victories being due to his terrific sprint. Many who saw Barras race, and, in particular, those who raced against him, believe if he'd been racing today Barras would have had a career similar to that of Mark Cavendish. There's merit in the belief too, the 1973 Tour of Switzerland is evidence of it.

In the early 1970s, teams could enter some European races, even those that are now part of the UCI World Tour, without racing regularly at that level. This wouldn't include the Tour de France, the Giro d'Italia and the Monuments, but did feature races like the Tour of Switzerland. Bantel didn't have enough members to qualify, but it was also possible for two teams to combine their riders. Bantel got together with British-based Holdsworth to take part in the 1973 Tour of Switzerland. Sid Barras was in the team, and he made history on day one.

After a short team time trial, the first stage ran from Zurich to Hanschiken. A group of thirty riders went clear early on the stage and most of them stayed clear. Sid Barras was in the breakaway, as was his Bantel teammate Reg Smith and Holdsworth-Campagnolo's Colin Lewis. Some fast European sprinters were in the break too, but none as fast as Barras. He hung on, over hill and dale, and galloped past everybody to win the stage.

Not only was Barras the first British cyclist ever to win a stage in the Tour of Switzerland, he took the yellow jersey, so he was the first to lead the race. That was a groundbreaking achievement and even now, after his long professional career, Barras remains proud. 'It wasn't a flat sprinter's stage, it was up and down all day. And it was good to wear the yellow jersey next day, it got us instant respect from the European pros,' Barras remembers.

He impressed a lot of people in European pro cycling with the way he raced in Switzerland. Raleigh wanted Barras for their team, TI-Raleigh, which at that time was taking on a growing European race programme. The aim was to take part in and win the biggest races, including the Tour de France, ideally with a team of British riders. Unfortunately for Barras, the man Raleigh chose to manage and develop the team from the end of 1973 onwards was the recently retired Dutch professional rider, Peter Post. Post was one of the best cyclists of his generation and had strong ideas about how a professional cycling team should be run. His ideas worked, and TI-Raleigh became the best team of its generation, but without any British riders. That's because Post had prejudices and one of them centred on British cyclists.

Lots of people have explanations as to why Post didn't like the British. The consensus seems to be that Post was jealous of Tom Simpson's 1965 road race world title victory. Whatever the reason, the Brits in the 1974 TI-Raleigh team felt they were given no encouragement, no guidance and were subject to petty and often bullying treatment by Post.

Sid Barras says, 'Right from the start, Post refused to recognise anything good we did, but was on top of us if we did anything wrong. I finished fifth in one of the big early season races in the south of France. I was the highest placed Raleigh rider by far, and the race had a really good field with all the big hitters in it, but Post said nothing to me afterwards, no congratulations, no "well done", nothing.'

Post's treatment grew worse, and most of the British TI-Raleigh riders in the European-based team went home to race with the UK-based half of the team. All but one never returned to top level European road racing or, if they did, it was only to take part in a handful of events. But even though they turned their back on the chance to perform at world level, many of them did very well and built great racing careers in the UK. Barras certainly did.

UK pro racing grew steadily throughout the 1970s and by the 1980s there was a thriving televised city-centre pro race series. It was sponsored by Kellogg's and other city-centre televised series followed. British professionals became very good at this fast, short, road-racing discipline, and although organisers paid top European riders – stars of the Tour de France, Giro d'Italia and other big races – to take part in them, they rarely won. Sid Barras won a lot.

Barras also excelled in road races, winning the British title in 1979 to add to his two circuit race national titles. He still rides his bike today and, even though he is now in his seventies, he's a leading figure in his local training groups that ride into and around the Yorkshire Dales. Sid Barras is as much a cycling legend for that as he was for his 380 professional race victories. He's always true to his racing nickname: 'Super Sid'.

Chapter Six
The Second Wave

The late 1970s saw a couple of British cyclists gain places in the biggest professional road race teams, and they were quickly followed by more during the next decade. By the end of the 1980s British men and women were racing and winning on the roads and in the velodromes of Europe again.

Paul Sherwen

7 June 1956 – 2 December 2018
First of the second wave of British cyclists in what is now the World Tour

Paul Sherwen racing in 1985

Paul Sherwen was born in Widnes, Lancashire, but grew up in Kenya. He returned to the UK as a teenager, took up cycling and studied at Manchester University. In 1976, Sherwen won the Pernod trophy in a competition where points were awarded according to finishing position in the top British amateur races. With its French sponsor the competition attracted attention in France and Sherwen was invited to race for a big Parisian club, the Athletic Club de Boulogne-Billancourt (ACBB) for the whole of 1977.

He did well, taking second place in the season-long Palme d'Or competition for amateur racers in France, despite having periods away from competition to complete his university studies in the UK. Second place was good enough to get Sherwen a contract with the Fiat professional team for 1978 and ACBB liked him so much they looked to the UK to find a replacement. The recruitment of English-speaking riders by ACBB, who subsequently became professionals with big French teams, had begun.

Sherwen was modest, self-deprecating and very witty. He told me, 'The Fiat team would have signed nearly anybody at the time I joined it. It had been created for and built around Eddy Merckx, with a two-year commitment to cycling team sponsorship by Fiat, but for some reason Merckx formed another team after the first year and took most of the Fiat riders with him. That left a team with all the equipment, bikes, cars and everything and no riders. We weren't exactly a gathering of big hitters in 1978.'

He looked back on his first year as a pro with fondness, though, especially at his very old-school team manager. 'It was an experience. Our manager was Raphael Geminiani, who'd been a great rider, but great riders don't always make great managers. He didn't believe in any frills and wouldn't supply arm or leg warmers to the team to help us race in cold conditions. We had to buy them if we wanted them. And I'll always remember what he said when I asked if we were getting waterproof jackets to wear if it rained in the cold early-season northern races. "You can't race with your coat on," he said. And that was it, no further explanation and no waterproof jackets.'

Sherwen remembered his first Tour de France too, and in particular some sage advice from seasoned pro Barry Hoban, which might have helped him survive an edition of the Tour quite a few far more experienced riders didn't. 'The 1978 Tour started on Saturday with a prologue time trial in the Dutch city of Leiden. Next day there were two stages, and I must have got some time bonuses or something in the morning stage, which gave me an outside chance of taking the yellow jersey if I could get some time bonuses or get away in a break during the afternoon. I went crazy.

'I was attacking all over the place, trying desperately to get a breakaway going, but it was nothing doing. I still kept trying, then Barry rode up alongside me and said, "What are you doing, Paul? You do know there are three more Sundays in this Tour de France."

'Suddenly I was confronted by how long the Tour was. Three more Sundays and I was racing flat out on the first. Seeing those three Sundays stretching out in front of me calmed me down no end. I'd have been wrecked in a week if I'd carried on like that, so I calmed down and hid in the peloton. It wasn't the last time Barry helped me that year either,' Sherwen told me during one of several interviews I did with him.

After two years with the Fiat team, Sherwen was established in top-level racing as a useful team rider who would contribute throughout a Tour de France and was competitive on his own right in northern European races. His best year was probably 1983, when racing for the Roubaix-based La Redoute-Motobecane team. Sherwen won the GP de Denain and was second overall in the Four Days of Dunkirk stage race.

After his European pro career ended Sherwen raced in the UK for a while, and became a team manager. He is most famous now for his off-the-bike career, when he formed a TV race commentating partnership with Phil Liggett. They were very good, playing to each other's strengths and eloquently describing races.

Cycling suffered a feeling of great loss when it was announced in 2018 that Paul Sherwen had passed away in his sleep at home in Uganda at the age of sixty-two. I was privileged to attend a packed memorial service for him in Manchester Cathedral and the respect and love inside that magnificent building could be felt, almost touched. It was a very moving experience and will stay with me for ever.

Graham Jones
Born 28 October 1957
Brilliant cyclist who could have been one of the best professionals of his time

Graham Jones taking part in the 1987 Tour de France

When they raced in the UK as amateurs, Paul Sherwen and Graham Jones were part of a talented south Manchester training group coached by Harold Nelson, who was something of a legend himself. Jones says, 'Harold – we all called him "H" – gave me, Paul Sherwen, then John Herety a great start in our racing careers. He was way ahead of his time and seemed to know things about training that sports scientists later discovered were very effective. For example, H understood that training at near the effort you could keep up in a one-hour time trial was a really potent way to build fitness. It was several years before scientists called that the anaerobic threshold and proved that training just below it was a very effective way to raise it and by doing so increase fitness.'

Jones's was the name Sherwen suggested at the end of 1977 when ACBB asked him to recommend a British cyclist to replace Sherwen in the club. Jones jumped at the chance: he'd wanted to be a professional in Europe almost since the day he took up the sport. Jones was a talented footballer with real prospects, but when he first saw photos of European racing in a 1970s magazine called *International Cycle Sport*, his true vocation jumped off the page at him. Without much experience, and still only seventeen, he found a family to lodge with in the Netherlands, and raced there for a while. Jones later spent the whole of 1977 racing in Belgium, where he made a big impression,

He was an instant hit with ACBB in 1978, going one better than Sherwen by winning the Palme d'Or competition outright. He won the two big French amateur time trials; the GP de France and the GP des Nations, the latter being recognised as the time trial world championships before the UCI created an official title race for the discipline. Jones also won several single day races, including Paris-Evreux, which was regarded as an amateur classic.

Those victories attracted the attention of the Peugeot professional team, which was a French cycling institution at the time and Jones was offered a place for 1979. It was the start of a trend that continued well into the 1980s – of English-speaking riders racing in France for ACBB, then becoming professionals for Peugeot.

Until 1978, Barry Hoban was the only British cyclist in a top European pro team, riding the biggest races for several years. Now he had two more Brits in the peloton with him. Paul Sherwen and Graham Jones both pay tribute to Hoban, not just for his achievements but for the help and advice he gave them, although Hoban, at heart a straight-talking Yorkshireman, was also quick to point out any mistakes they made. 'He was quite hard on us at times,' Jones says. 'For example, I remember once when Paul punctured in a race and Barry just told him he should look where he was going because punctures are a rider's fault for not seeing hazards.'

Jones made a good pro debut and, in 1980, he looked set to join the top echelons of the sport when he made his Tour de France debut. He was lying eleventh overall in that Tour with just one mountain stage and a time trial to go, and fancied his chances of ending up even higher in Paris. However, it wasn't to be. 'I think I was the only rider up till then who had won the two classic amateur time trials; the GP de France and GP des Nations in the same year.

The Second Wave

So, with only a time trial stage left after one in the mountains, and I'd been climbing well, I was confident I could finish in the first ten overall by the end. But several of us in the Peugeot team caught some sort of stomach bug before that final mountain stage, so I was dropped early in the stage and had to ride a hundred kilometres – up and over two big mountain passes – on my own and behind everybody. I was empty,' he says.

Jones plummeted down the overall standings and ended up forty-ninth overall by the time the race finished. His career would have been so much different if he'd gained that top ten in his first Tour de France. It would have earned him status within the sport and within his team. Jones would have become a protected rider with teammates working for him in some races. Instead, he had to work for them. What made things worse was Jones was good in all kinds of terrain and all kinds of races, so Peugeot picked him for everything.

Treating Jones like that was very short-sighted. In 1981 he finished second in the Tour of the Mediterranean, having beaten no less than Bernard Hinault. He was brilliant again in the Critérium International, a two-day, three-stage race. He attacked Hinault when the five-time Tour de France-winning Frenchman led overall, and Hinault had to get all his teammates to ride hard to contain Jones. But then fate took a hand again, when Jones collided with a camera motorbike on a descent as it looked like he might win. Another chance to improve his status in European pro cycling had gone.

Jones crashed on a training ride early the following year and broke a femur. The enforced lay-off probably did him good, though, because he was a notorious hard trainer. His racing season kicked off with second place in Het Volk which was good, performing well in a cobbled classic after his great Tour de France debut. This should have flagged up Jones's potential to Peugeot, but it didn't. The team kept putting him in every race, and it was wearing him out.

Jones has regrets about letting the team do that now, blaming himself. Robert Millar (see next entry, Pippa York), another British cycling legend, joined the Peugeot team in 1980 and Jones told me, 'If they picked Robert for a race that didn't suit him he just told them he wouldn't ride. It didn't always make him a popular teammate, but it meant he only rode the races that suited him, and that helped develop his talent. And in the end popularity didn't matter. When Robert started winning big mountain stages in the Tour, and began to look like a contender overall, nobody complained about him. But you needed confidence to do what Robert did back then, and I didn't have that confidence. I regret it now, but it can't be changed,' Jones says.

Racing up to 150 days a year eventually took its toll. Jones became exhausted and returned to live in the UK, racing for a British-based pro team. He did OK, but it was a big step down, and he wasn't comfortable with it.

Jones had his fair share of bad luck – but for a stomach bug, tenth place overall in his first Tour de France was on the cards, and that would have seen his career take a different path. But still, he made it as a British cyclist at the top of world cycling, became part of a big pro team and rode the biggest races. It was exceptionally hard to do that when Jones did it. Many tried, but few were called.

Graham Jones was called, he did well and he should be proud of that; British cycling certainly is.

Pippa York

**Born 13 September 1958
First British King of the Mountains title-holder and highest Tour de France finisher before Bradley Wiggins**

Pippa York, then Robert Millar, taking part in the 1986 Tour de France

Pippa York was born and competed as Robert Millar. She is from Glasgow and grew up in the Gorbals, a place that knew hardship, but many residents remember the feeling of genuine community spirit.

Like many young people, York used cycling to discover the wider world and especially the stunning countryside around her home city. She joined Glenmarnock Wheelers Cycling Club and started racing, winning the Scottish junior road race championships in 1976 and the Scottish senior hill climb championships the following year.

In 1978, and still only nineteen, York won the British amateur road race championships on a hilly circuit in the Lincolnshire Wolds. She won easily too, beating the best amateur road racers in the UK, the majority of whom were older and far more experienced. The French club ACBB was monitoring British amateur road racing for successors to Paul Sherwen and Graham Jones and offered York a place for 1979.

She was a great success, winning five big French races and the season-long competition to find the country's best amateur road racer. York also finished fourth in the amateur road race world championships and might have won but for a mechanical problem in the final few hundred metres of the race.

York turned pro for Peugeot in 1980 with the conviction that her gift for riding quickly up any kind of hill would take her a long way in cycling. Races like the Tour de France and the other Grand Tours are decided by performance in the high mountains and York could perform. But climbing is a fragile gift that requires nurturing. York was single-minded about doing that.

From the start of her pro career she focused only on the races that helped her develop the way she knew she had to, and consistently finished top ten overall in major, week-long stage races. By 1983 she was ready for the Tour de France and taking second place overall in the Critérium du Dauphiné to a future Tour winner – Greg LeMond – secured her a place in the Peugeot Tour team for York. Grand Tours were York's forte and she made a great Tour de France debut in 1983. It was slightly marred by a crash on stage three, which might have cost York a top ten placing, but she still finished fourteenth overall and sealed her future on a stage in the Pyrenees. York attacked on the Col du Tourmalet, one of the most famous mountain climbs in Tour de France history, caught the one rider who was ahead, and crossed the summit alone. York kept enough of her summit gap on the rest while descending into Luchon, where the stage finished. At the end York was still six seconds ahead of a Spanish future Tour winner, Pedro Delgado. She became the fourth British cyclist in history to win a Tour de France stage.

York was established now and the following year had her best-ever Tour de France. After contending in Paris–Nice, Tour of Romandy and the Midi Libre stage races, either winning or finishing near the front on the biggest mountain stages, she won another stage in the Tour. She was a joy to watch, climbing beautifully. York is lightly built; her power-to-weight ratio couldn't be measured when she raced, as can be done with riders today, but it must have been incredible. She ended the 1984 Tour in fourth place overall, the highest overall placing by any British cyclist in the Tour until Sir Bradley Wiggins's third place in 2009. That year she also became the first British cyclist to win the mountains competition in the Tour de France or any Grand Tour for that matter.

York was one of the best climbers the sport has ever seen and in her day a favourite to win any Grand Tour she rode. Until the penultimate stage it looked like she would win the 1985 Vuelta a España. She took the lead on stage ten, holding a ten-second lead over Francisco Rodriguez and she was over a minute ahead of third-placed Pello Ruiz Cabestany. Neither could climb like York, although Rodriguez kept attacking her on that penultimate stage. York nullified everything her Spanish rivals tried, but then punctured at the start of a climb. She quickly caught the group she was riding in and stayed there, thinking all the contenders were with her. Some riders even started congratulating her, on the face of it accepting the fact that York had the race sewn up, but she hadn't. It was a trick.

A few riders had gone ahead of York's group and two of the escapees, who were both Spanish, were in a position to threaten her overall lead. The thing is nobody told York, the breakaway wasn't announced on race radio and even her manager, following the race in the Peugeot team car, didn't know what was happening.

The dangerous attackers were José Recio and Pedro Delgado, both rivals because they raced for different teams. The stage covered some of Delgado's home roads, and he was only six minutes behind York in the overall standings. He took most of that time back before York found out what was happening. The British rider went straight to the front of the group to set the pace, but nobody would help her. In contrast, Delgado had Recio working with him up front, and they gained another thirty-six seconds on York by the stage finish.

York was appalled at what happened and just as unimpressed with the spirit of the whole race. This is how she summed the race up in an interview with *Winning* magazine: 'The crowds throw things at you and spit at you because they want a Spaniard to win.

But I don't let them affect me; I still get on and race. The other night, though, at the hotel in Albacete, I blew my top. We had been waiting an hour for dinner, and when it came it was food you wouldn't give your dog. The others couldn't believe it when I stormed out. I went down to the cake shop and stuffed myself.

'Next day, the whole Fagor team attacked with Delgado at the first feed because they thought I was hungry. I had planned for our team to ride through both feeds to make the others hungry, but the guys said they were hot and wanted their feeds. The Spanish riders lost the race for me, but I'll get my own back on them.'

Neither was York happy with the Peugeot team manager, Roland Berland. He'd been a pro racer himself for many years and would know how nationalistic the Vuelta and the Giro d'Italia still were back then. Spanish and Italian riders would unite if any foreigner looked like winning. Berland should have expected a plot and been on the lookout, but he wasn't.

Also, Peugeot was never a well organised team. The mechanics hadn't even brought York's time trial bike with them to Spain. Once she was contending for victory the bike had to be flown from France so she could defend her lead in the time trials. Neglect like that really knocks a rider's confidence

It's no surprise that York moved to the highly organised Dutch Panasonic team the following year, although she wasn't exactly the best fit with its manager, Peter Post. Post had his way of doing things, but so did York. They didn't see eye to eye on a number of things, and neither would compromise, which resulted in several arguments, and a couple of really bizarre ones – the bizarreness all on Post's side. But Post respected York's ability, and they had good results together, including another second place overall in the Vuelta a España and second overall in the 1987 Giro d'Italia as well as the climber's prize in that race, another first for a UK rider.

The 1987 Giro showed another side of Pippa York, when she wholeheartedly helped the Irish rider Stephen Roche in his successful attempt to win the race. Roche had taken the lead from an Italian teammate, but in doing so incurred the wrath of the *Tifosi*, the fans who were fiercely loyal to Italian riders. Roche was in a different team to York, so was a rival, but on the mountain stage, after Roche took the lead, she rode to protect the Irishman. She and Roche's Dutch teammate Eddy Schepers rode either side of him, stopping any fan who might want to impede Roche's progress.

York's pro cycling career continued until 1995 and she won races like the Tour of Britain in 1989 and the 1990 Critérium du Dauphiné. She had high places in other big races, but also became a very good team rider. York played a key support role in the 1990 Tour de France which helped teammate Greg LeMond win the race.

Looking back, though, it's hard to believe that throughout her brilliant career, and through the whole of the first part of her life, York was unhappy with her identity as Robert Millar. After she stopped cycling she slowly slipped out of the public eye, but now she's back and making a big and very valued contribution to our enjoyment of cycling today, with her work for a number of media platforms.

Sean Yates

Born 18 May 1960
First British cyclist to win a Tour de France time trial stage

Sean Yates in the yellow jersey (left) riding with Chris Boardman in the 1994 Tour de France

ACBB didn't just recruit British cyclists and feed them into the Peugeot professional team. From outside France in the 1980s, Phil Anderson and Allan Peiper of Australia both graduated through the grey-and-orange ACBB kit to the Peugeot black-and-white (the pro team and amateur club were linked by Cycles Peugeot sponsorship and its distinctive chequered motif). The Irish rider, Stephen Roche was another very successful ACBB-to-Peugeot graduate.

Sean Yates followed that path from Sussex. He was a powerfully built rider who excelled at time trials and in the individual and team pursuit disciplines as an amateur. His original cycling ambition was to race in the Olympic Games, which he did in Moscow in 1980, but after that says, 'I felt I owed it to my dad, who'd given me so much support, to push onwards and upwards. Dad was a fan of European professional road racing and had been for a long time. He was a big supporter of Tom Simpson in the 1960s, so because of him more than anything I decided try to become professional in Europe.'

Yates's local bike shop owner, Tony Mills – a pro rider in the sixties who raced in Europe – managed to get him an invitation to the 1980 amateur GP des Nations in France, where Yates finished second. Stephen Roche won that race for ACBB and because Roche had a place in the Peugeot team for 1981, Yates replaced him. By 1981 ACBB's love of British cyclists had gone into overdrive. Three others also rode for the French club that year: John Herety, Jeff Williams and Kevin Reilly. As Yates recalls, 'Having four of us was much better than it was for the first British pros, who went to Europe alone. It really helped us, and we did OK. I won the GP de France time trial and that was really important because a contact with the Peugeot pro team came straight after. I sort of fell into it.'

John Herety graduated into the Coop-Mercier professional team and had some very good placings in big European pro races, as well as winning the 1982 British pro road race title. Yates, though, had a much longer European pro career, even though it had a slower start. He began to spark as a pro rider when Allan Peiper joined Peugeot in 1983. Peiper was more driven than the laidback Yates, and more organised. However, they became close friends and, over time, something of Peiper rubbed off onto Yates. By 1984, when they did their first Tour de France together, they were almost inseparable and a real force in the Peugeot team.

Peiper recalls, 'Me and Sean were mad keen on time trials. We researched the best equipment and the best ways to train for them and we dragged Peugeot to fourth place in the 1984 Tour team time trial. We then spent the rest of that Tour doing anything we could for Pippa York, who ended up fourth overall. Once the Tour ended, Sean and I had twenty-five straight days of racing in critériums, travelling all over Europe together. It was a very special time for us. It didn't seem like work at all, just two young men on an adventure. It was an incredibly free time; we had nothing, so we had nothing to lose.'

It was an adventure, but Peiper, free spirit though he was, was also driven to explore his own potential and left Peugeot to join the better organised Panasonic team. Yates drifted a little on his own with Peugeot, and the team let him go when his contract with them ended, so he joined the much smaller Franco/Spanish Fagor team.

It looked like a step down, but it coincided with a big change in his life that helped him become a much better rider.

Yates examined his life and decided that, as a young single man with no ties, but having a European employer, he could live where he wanted, opted for the sun and moved to Nice. He'd lived at home or shared accommodation with other riders so far in his life; now he was living alone for the first time. Not knowing many people in his new city, Yates filled his time with more cycling, plus lots more relaxing – albeit on the beach – which meant more training and better recovery.

He explains his choices: 'I really love cycling, I still do, so I spent endless hours riding the back roads and the hills behind the coast. When I got home there was nothing to eat, so I'd shower and go out to eat, and doing that meant I ate a lot less and lost quite a bit of weight, so when I rode for the Fagor team I started riding a lot better.'

Yates had found the key to being a good pro: accumulate hours on the bike, add recovery time and restrict eating to what's needed, and you get much fitter and stronger. It's the way to unlock the key to success in cycling, a high power to weight ration. Yates had already built a reputation as a reliable domestique with Peugeot and his increased power and a lighter body meant Yates now got results for himself.

In 1987 he won the GP de Cannes and a stage in Ireland's Nissan Classic, then really stepped up in 1988, winning stages in Paris–Nice and the Vuelta a España. He also scored his career-crowning victory that year by taking a time trial stage in the Tour de France, becoming the first British cyclist ever to win a Tour de France time trial.

Yates won a total of thirty professional races during his long career, the final half of which – 1989 to 1996 – was spent with American teams: 7-Eleven then Motorola. Although he was a proven winner, Yates says he was still happier working for others. He was so good and so valued, he'd moved into a bracket of very well-paid team support riders called the 'super-domestiques'.

Not in every race though: Yates still challenged when the terrain suited him, and he had some high placings in the Monument Paris–Roubaix. It was also great when in 1993, just for one day, Sean Yates became the third British cyclist ever to wear the yellow jersey in the Tour de France. It was like the yellow jersey was Yates's long service and good conduct medal. Not only was all of British cycling happy for him, but so was the multi-national professional peloton.

Sean Yates was popular and respected when he raced, and he took that with him when he moved into team management. He was very successful, young riders liked working with him, they appreciated his no-nonsense attitude and how he saw clearly through the chaos of a bike race.

Yates was the number one sports director with Team Sky for several years, and it was a high point for both of them when, in 2012, Sir Bradley Wiggins became the first British cyclist to win the Tour de France. Sean Yates had directed things from the Sky team car and deserves credit for what he did to help create that very special piece of British cycling history.

Tony Doyle
19 May 1958 – 23 April 2023
Britain's best ever six-day racer;
double world champion

Tony Doyle (left) racing in a Madison at the 1991 Grenoble six-day race

Tony Doyle was one of the best six-day racers in the world at a time when six-day racing was a big attraction, and big business. There are fewer of these events each year, and they don't stand comparison with the past in terms of atmosphere and attraction. It was very different when Tony Doyle raced in the 1980s and 1990s, the final days of the golden era of six-day racing.

Doyle was born in Ashford, Middlesex. His first cycling experiences were with Clarence Wheelers, a London cycling club with a reputation for developing talented time triallists on the road and great individual and team pursuit racers on the track. Tony Doyle was both.

He turned professional after the 1980 Olympic Games in Moscow, where he competed in the team pursuit. It was a disappointing Olympics for Doyle who, as reigning British champion in the individual pursuit, had expected to ride that event at the Games, but the selectors picked Sean Yates instead. A few weeks later Doyle threw that decision into question when he won the 1980 professional pursuit world title. He would win the pro pursuit world title again in 1986, but it was six-day racing where really Doyle left his mark.

Before Doyle only Tom Simpson and a Londoner, Tony Gowland, had won a modern six-day race. Where Simpson won one and Gowland two, Doyle won twenty six-days during his career and no other British rider has come anywhere near than number.

Modern six-days revolve around Madison races, two-man team constant relays in which one rider races while the other laps more slowly around the outside of the track. They change places with a hefty hand-sling, where the rider who had been racing literally throws the one who has been lapping around the outside of the track into the action. It's fast, spectacular and very skilful racing. There are other races apart from Madisons in a six-day race, such as motor-paced races and sprints, but the Madisons are the most important factor, the core of six-day, where the race is decided.

Madison racing is a track endurance race and the best Madison teams are made up of a rider who can sprint and has plenty of stamina and one who might have a lower top-end speed but can ride hard, lap after lap. The 2012 Tour de France winner Sir Bradley Wiggins, a great pursuit and time-trial rider and Mark Cavendish, one of the best road sprinters of all time, were a fabulous Madison pairing, for example.

After showing great flair, stamina and dependability, Tony Doyle formed a regular partnership with the Australian Danny Clarke, and it was perfect. Clarke was one of the fastest men of his era and they dominated six-day racing for a while. In 1983 they won their first six-days, the Berlin and Dortmund events, then in 1985 Doyle won in Bremen with Garry Wiggins, Sir Bradley's Australian father. After that Doyle was Clarke's regular partner, and they won sixteen six-days together.

'We were so successful the six-day promoters started splitting us up in their races, pairing us with different riders so we didn't dominate things, or so they said. I think another reason was that Danny [Clarke] was getting close to Patrick Sercu's all-time record of eighty-two six-days. Sercu is Belgian and I think there was a bit of European pride involved; they didn't want Danny to break Sercu's record. In the end Danny won seventy-seven six-days, but he could have won more together if the promotors had paired him with me more often.'

Doyle took his career six-day total to a final tally of twenty victories in 1991, when he was partnered with local hero Etienne De Wilde in the Ghent Six-Day. Doyle wasn't quite the rider he had been by then, though, because he'd had a long and difficult fight to return to racing after a terrible, life-threatening crash during the 1989 Munich Six-Day race.

In the fast, exciting world of six-day track racing the riders have to be incredibly skilled, as well as fit and fast. To preserve the spectacle, the competitors have to race as though they trust each other implicitly. For most of the time that works; each rider trusts the skills and judgement of the others, but human beings do make mistakes. But a mistake made when everybody is racing full on in a six-day can have disastrous consequences. In Munich in 1989 one of Doyle's fellow competitors made a mistake, and it was disastrous for Doyle.

He collided with the rider and was flung from his bike and knocked unconscious. Doyle suffered multiple fractures and a serious head injury that left him in a coma for ten days. For a while it was touch-and-go if he'd survive. Doyle eventually spent six weeks in an intensive care unit, followed by two months in a rehabilitation centre, building his body back.

Very few thought he'd be able to race again, but he went on to win two more six-days, including that final one with De Wilde in Ghent. He continued until 1994, until a crash during the Zurich Six-Day, in which he broke his back, finally ended his racing career.

Doyle stayed in cycling. He was president of the British Cycling Federation for a short time and played an important role in implementing long-needed changes that led to the creation of British

The Second Wave

Cycling, the sport's UK governing body. He died in 2023, just four weeks after being diagnosed with pancreatic cancer. The British Cycling that Tony Doyle left was far fitter and better able to govern than the one he joined. There are many reasons why Tony Doyle is a British cycling legend, not just confined to the speed with which he pedalled a bike.

Mandy Jones
Born 24 March 1962
First British road race world champion after Beryl Burton

Mandy Jones winning the 1982 road race world title in Goodwood

Mandy Jones was born in Rochdale, Lancashire, close by the Pennine Hills. She comes from a cycling family, her mother and father were active members of the West Pennine Cycling Club. They enrolled Mandy when she was ten and old enough to ride with them. She was quickly followed by her younger sister, Carol.

Cycling was a big family activity for the Joneses, with regular club runs and family cycle-camping holidays around the beauty spots of northern England, including the Lake District. Mandy showed promise in a few local time trials and began doing training rides. She tried road racing at sixteen and from those first few races her rise to prominence was meteoric. Her ability and talent quickly exceeded her experience and her resources, as she explains. 'There was no lottery funding when I raced like there is now. Everything you had – your bikes and clothing – were yours or in my case my mum and dad's because they got me my first quality race bike.'

That first quality race bike was too big for her: 'Maybe my dad thought I would grow into it,' Jones says. Size aside, the bike took Mandy Jones a long way. Still only eighteen she was selected to ride for the British team at the 1980 road race world championships, held on a very hilly circuit based on the town of Sallanches in the Alps. The best in the world were there, most of them riding custom-built bikes provided by their personal sponsors or by their national cycling federations, but Mandy Jones on her too-big-bike was more than a match for them.

She was sensational. By riding strongly at or near the front of the race she got into the winning breakaway and some of the biggest names in cycling were in it with her. 'The thing is,' she says, 'There was no information beforehand from the British Cycling Federation about the course and there was this long, steep hill to do every lap. All the others in the breakaway knew about it and had an extra-low gear fitted, but I just had the normal gear ratios I'd used in any other race. I struggled up that hill on every lap and had to catch up on the descent.' She caught up well, though, taking third place – a bronze medal in her first world championship and she was still in her teens.

Mandy Jones was special, her family could see it and they supported her training full-time, which was what she needed to do to step up from bronze to gold. Many of Jones's sessions were done with two local male professional racers, Jack Kershaw and Ian Greenhalgh, who made no concession on their rides. It was a tough school.

Today, Jones pays tribute to her parents for their support during that period, recognising that it was part of the reason for her success. 'There wasn't the sponsorship to go full-time, my only "sponsorship" came from registering as unemployed, "going on the dole", as we called it, and from my mum and dad. We talked about it, though, talked about the choices; either I could go full-time training and racing for a while, with their help, and do everything I could for when the world championships were in the UK in 1982, or get a part-time job and miss out on some training and perhaps not be as good as I could be. They decided to support me so I'd have every chance of winning the worlds that year.'

After a further year of steady improvement and some very good results in 1981, in 1982 Jones became the first woman to beat Beryl

Burton in any national time trial championships for over twenty years. However, in the final run-up she made a mistake while she was training for her target discipline, the one in which she felt she had the best chance of winning a world title.

'I liked time trials best when I was racing. I was a strong rider, and where a weaker rider might be able to hang on to a stronger one in a road race then outsprint them at the end, they can't do that in a time trial. There wasn't a time trial world championship when I raced, but there was the individual pursuit on the track, which is a short time trial really. I targeted the pursuit for the 1982 worlds, when the track events were held in Leicester and the road races at Goodwood. But I didn't know so much about training and preparation and I kept training hard in the week running up to it. In the end I didn't ride the pursuit as well as I could have. I could ride faster than I did, but I was tired because I'd been training hard right up to it.

'At the time I thought, well, that's that, no world title, and I just kicked back. I took it easy for a few days before the road races. I thought I'd missed my chance, but by kicking back I was letting my body recover from all the training I'd done. I got the benefit of the training I'd done in the road race, instead of on the track.'

Training hard then backing off – 'tapering', as it's called now – is how all athletes achieve peak form. Coaches and cyclists know that now, but not everybody knew when Jones was racing. A lot of athletes self-sabotage, losing confidence in the run-up to a target race, and think they need to keep training to get fitter and stronger. Essentially, they are panic training up to the event because they dare not ease off, thinking they might lose some fitness.

There were a few days between the women's individual pursuit in Leicester and the women's road race on the Goodwood circuit in Sussex. By taking it easy on those days, Mandy Jones was tapering her training without realising it, which meant her body could

The Second Wave

respond to the hard training she'd done and build up its reserves. On the day of the race, she was well rested, totally recovered and in fantastic form. Her world title victory ended up being fairly straightforward.

'I got in a breakaway on the last lap with Maria Canins of Italy, Sandra Schumacher of France and a Belgian, Gerda Sierens, but how I got away from them to win was a bit strange, because it wasn't an attack. I just pedalled around a corner and the others freewheeled round it. It was at the start of the downhill and I looked behind me and saw I had a gap. I don't know if they didn't see me, but they relaxed and I thought, Just get down this hill fast. I was away, and with all the solo time trialling I'd done I was in my element.

'The course was very twisty, so pretty soon the riders I'd been in the break with lost sight of me. It stayed that way until we got onto the Goodwood motor-racing circuit for the last time. It's a wide, open circuit, and they could see me there. It's not nice leading like that: you are alone in front and can see across the circuit, and see them working together. I didn't have a big lead, so I thought with them all working together, and how good they were, there's absolutely no chance of me staying away. Still, I just kept going – there was nothing else I could do; I was committed. We came to the hill for the last time, the finish was near the top, and I was still ahead. I only had ten seconds lead, but I just gave it all I'd got and I hung on to win.'

She'd become road race world champion and race world champion and Mandy Jones was still only twenty. Her future looked very bright, but things weren't as straightforward for British cyclists as they are now. Jones would be part of a highly organised professional team today, racing all over the world and getting paid well for doing so. But in the 1980s, world champion or not, British women needed family or other independent support to train and race full-time. They were also very much on their own when deciding what training and racing to do.

Most professional cycling teams today have highly qualified coaches who create individualised training programmes. Skilled practitioners keep riders in top physical condition and many teams have doctors, nutritionists and even psychologists who work with the riders to ensure that they develop as they should. Mandy Jones had none of that. She trained hard and picked up a calf injury that took a number of years to rectify.

During the 1990s, British cyclists who were at Olympic level started getting some of this back-up support, and Jones finally got her injury treated successfully. However, her life had changed by then, and once her injury was gone she felt it was too close to the next Olympics to continue racing. She still cycles whenever she can, and she's still a legend; always will be.

Maurice Burton

25 October 1955
First black British champion;
first black cyclist in international professional six-day racing

Maurice Burton at the 2015 London six-day race, where he was supporting his son Germain

Maurice Burton was born and grew up in south London. His father was born in Jamaica and, looking for greater opportunities than life offered on the island, travelled with his brother to work in the US for a while before returning home. He then sailed to the UK on the first ship that left after the *Empire Windrush*, part of the early wave of people from the West Indies who made a new life.

Mr Burton did well here. He became a tailor specialising in men's suit alterations and worked in London's West End. He married, and was ambitious for his young son, Maurice. He wanted him to become a doctor or a lawyer, but his son discovered a different ambition. This is what he once told me about it.

'I think it was 1970 or '71 when I got hold of a colour magazine that covered European pro cycling, races like the Classics and the Tour de France, and I couldn't put it down. I was fascinated by what was in it, the stories of the races and the photos of Eddy Merckx and the rest. I didn't know that world existed before picking up that magazine, but I wanted to be part of it.'

But it wasn't what his father wanted, and he refused to buy Maurice a bike, who found one instead. 'I was coming home from school and I saw this bike in a front garden. It looked like it had been thrown out, it was a bit knocked about. I went to this house, knocked on the door and asked if I could have it. The woman there said I could, so I took the bike, fixed it up and that was my first race bike.'

His next stop was London's Herne Hill Velodrome, with coached training sessions and lots of races. Burton was a natural, winning almost every time. By 1973 he was beating senior riders and won the British junior track sprint championships that year. It was Burton's first national title and the first time a black cyclist had ever won a British championships.

Burton's coach at Herne Hill encouragingly told him that he was starting his journey to the Olympic Games. But Burton encountered racism right from the start. Some riders grew angry when he beat them – and they didn't when they were beaten by white riders. The most overt and shameful exhibition came in 1974, when the eighteen-year-old Burton won his first senior national title. It was the twenty-kilometre track race and Burton won easily, outsprinting the reigning Commonwealth Games gold medallist by some distance. Burton was delighted, he was presented with his gold medal and national champion's jersey, but when he raised his victory bouquet into the air some in the crowd booed.

It was a terrible response to a young athlete who had just won a big race, and Burton's reaction to the booing does him credit. During an interview I did with him for a cycling magazine I asked him how the incident made him feel. He was young and impressionable, so I thought it might have damaged him in some way, but no: 'I felt sorry for them to be honest. I mean, they were grown men booing a teenager who had won a big race. I won fair and I won well, so the only reason they were booing was because I was black. I remember thinking, You've got the problem, mate, I haven't got a problem.'

Burton was selected to represent England at the 1974 Commonwealth Games, but was unexpectedly left off the squad riders long-listed for the Olympic Games two years later. That was despite having consistently beaten and proved himself faster than others on the list. It doesn't take much imagination to come up with the reason for his omission.

Undeterred, Burton continued following his ambition to become a professional cyclist in Europe. 'I only wanted to go to the Olympics because I knew if I did something there it would help me get a contract with a professional team. I wasn't in cycling for medals, I wanted to make money, and to do that you had to be a pro in Europe,' he says. Burton moved to Ghent, Belgium, and tried to become a professional rider by being part of racing on the continent.

It worked. Racing summers on the road and winters on the track, Burton broke into the world professional six-day racing. It was a tough school, the racing was hard, fast and long. Pro six-days were a real spectacle and the knowledgeable crowds who flocked to see them wouldn't tolerate easy racing.

Burton not only survived in this world, but thrived. He lived in Europe for ten years and took part in fifty-six six-days, which meant he was an accepted regular. This was tough in a world where contracts to take part are awarded on a race-to-race basis. A rider had to be consistently good and Burton only didn't win a six-day because he was used by promotors as a circuit 'taxi driver'. That meant he was safe, reliable and could be paired with the most inexperienced riders in the race. Not a path to glory maybe, but it kept Burton in work and well paid.

He was part of something in Europe, highly respected, and today he can look back with pride on being part of the circuit when six-days were really something in cycling. Burton raced against all the greats of his era, including Eddy Merckx, and was accepted as an equal by them. A bad crash in a race in Argentina eventually ended his career, but not his love of cycling. After achieving success in business, Burton still rides his bike as much as he possibly can and enjoys every minute of it.

Malcolm Elliott

Born 1 July 1961
First British cyclist to win the
points jersey in a Grand Tour

Malcom Elliott in 2017

Sheffield's Malcolm Elliott is famous in cycling for several reasons; his impeccable riding style, his fearsome sprint, a sprint that earned him three stage wins in the Vuelta a España as the points jersey in that race and for the longevity of his professional cycling career. Not only was he a pro from 1984 until 1997, but he returned to the sport in 2003 at the age of forty-one and continued racing at elite level, and winning, until he was fifty.

Elliott joined the Rutland Cycling Club in Sheffield at the age of fifteen. He started racing and started winning. His first senior national title – the men's hill climb – came in 1980, when he also raced for a French cycling club in Troyes. Elliott was as good at track cycling as he was on the road and was selected to represent Great Britain in the track team pursuit event at the 1980 Olympic Games in Moscow.

There was no medal for Elliott in Moscow, but he won two golds – in the road race and the team time trial – at the 1982 Commonwealth Games in Brisbane, Australia. His amateur racing career ended with him winning six stages and the overall classification of the 1983 Milk Race Tour of Britain.

Elliott spent the next three years competing in the growing number of British professional races, but he was good enough for a place in European pro road racing, as he proved when he joined the ANC-Halfords team. ANC-Halfords was British, but in 1987 it made the step up to compete in the biggest European pro races, including the Tour de France.

Elliott was twenty-five and quickly proved that he had the talent to be with the best. ANC-Halfords took part in as many top-level European races as they could, and Elliott gave the team its best results. He was part of the four-man winning breakaway in the Amstel Gold Race in the Netherlands.

Amstel Gold Race is a classic, a tough race that only the best win. Elliott loved it; he'd trained in the hilly Peak District of Derbyshire and south Yorkshire ever since he started cycling and it was great preparation for the brutal course in the hilly region of Holland. Elliott was near the front of the peloton all day and towards the end he was one of the three riders who had enough left in their legs to follow Tour de France King of the Mountains Steven Rooks when he attacked up the slopes of the most famous climb in the race, the Cauberg. The other two who went with him were the 1980 Tour de France winner, Joop Zoetemelk and a talented young Dutch rider called Teun van Vliet.

The breakaway quickly gained enough time to stay clear until the end, but the three Dutch riders seemed to understand that Elliott was by far the best sprinter in the group and maybe national pride rather than personal ambition decided how they played things. Joop Zoetemelk attacked three kilometres from the finish, and the two remaining Dutch riders didn't chase him. Elliott did chase, but when he asked the two Dutch riders to help him they refused.

After the race Elliott admitted he wasn't strong enough to chase on his own. And in the end he had been too exhausted to follow Steven Rooks when he attacked in the final kilometres to take second place behind Zoetemelk. Elliott had to be content with third, but third place in Amstel Gold is good and a lot of European teams noted Elliott's name.

The Second Wave

ANC-Halfords continued racing in Europe and did enough to impress the Tour de France organisers, who included the team in their line-up for the 1987 race. The Tour was a difficult time for the team, though – not because the riders weren't good enough, but because the team's funding ran out during the race. The three riders who got to the end in Paris only did so because their team manager, Phil Griffiths, had plenty of leeway left on his credit cards and used it to pay the team's way.

Elliott was one of the three who made it to the end and he showed he could contend for sprint stage wins with a few high placings, including third on the stage to Bordeaux. When ANC-Halfords disbanded, he was offered a one-year contract by the Spanish Fagor team and won his first Grand Tour stage for them in the 1988 Vuelta a España.

Elliott liked racing in Spain and joined another Spanish team, Teka, in 1989, winning two stages and the points jersey in the Vuelta a España. It was the first time a British cyclist had won a points jersey outright in any Grand Tour. Elliot continued racing for Spanish teams in Europe until the end of 1992, taking a number of stage wins in prestigious races like the Tour of the Basque Country and Volta a Catalunya.

Professional cycling was as popular as ever in Europe in Elliott's time, but during the second half of the 1980s and into the nineties the sport grew rapidly in the US as well. America's Greg LeMond created interest at home by winning the professional road race world title twice and the Tour de France three times, the first American to do so. Several big races with good prize money were created in the US and a growing number of US-based pro teams took part in them.

In 1993, Elliott joined one of these new US teams, Chevrolet-LA Sheriffs, and moved to California. He was one of the first British cyclists to relocate and was quickly followed by others. Elliott soon became one of the best US pros, winning the prestigious First Union Grand Prix in 1993 and 1994, as well as the Redlands Classic in those two years. He also won stages in the 1993 and 1995 Tour du Pont, which was one of the US races favoured by many top European pro teams. Unfortunately, the US growth bubble began to deflate during the second half of the 1990s and Elliott decided to retire from his pro cycling career in 1997 at the age of thirty-six, when he had plenty of racing left in him.

Returning to Sheffield, he got on with life outside of pro cycling, but the desire to race and in particular to train, to ride his bike with a purpose again, never really went away. He started training again with a view to taking part in some age-group races. In doing so, he rediscovered the profound love of cycling in the Peak District he'd first encountered as a teenager with the Rutland Cycling Club. Elliott returned to racing aged forty-one, quite casually at first, but he was soon winning races and quickly returned to professional – or, as it was called by then – elite level racing.

Elliott admits that during his first racing career – in his teens to his thirties – he wasn't the most dedicated cyclist. He had so much talent that he could win without training as much as others and living a monk-like existence. But when he returned, he spent as much time on long rides as he could squeeze between other commitments. He also says he felt so much better physically and mentally because of it. At the back of his mind, he wondered just what he could have won if he'd had the same enthusiasm and dedication to training during his first racing career. I feel he certainly would have won some really big races.

Representing a series of British teams, he won the UK season-long competition to find the most consistent road racer in the country, the Premier Calendar, as well as the National Elite Circuit

Series in 2004. In 2007 he won the UCI 1.2 ranked single-day race and the International CiCle Classic, as well as many other races. However, those victories were almost an aside: I think Malcolm Elliott's real victory was rediscovering the simple joy of cycling that he had experienced as a fifteen-year-old exploring the Peak District with the Rutland Cycling Club.

Colin Sturgess

**Born 15 December 1968
Claimed world pursuit
champion title aged twenty**

Colin Sturgess in a cycling
magazine photoshoot

Winning a professional world title at the age of twenty in 1989, when training knowledge wasn't as deep as it is now, was remarkable. Today, every possible metric is measured; back then, riders used to have to explore what worked for them. The achievement was a real testament to Colin Sturgess's prodigious talent.

Colin Sturgess was an exception, but the fact that he didn't become one of the best pro cyclists of his generation was, to a certain extent, a reflection of what was going on in pro cycling when he started making his way in it.

Sturgess was born in Ossett, west Yorkshire, the son of Alan and Anne Sturgess, who had both been top level cyclists. The family moved to Johannesburg in South Africa when Colin was six, where Colin started cycling. He progressed well, but his parents saw opportunities to race internationally, particularly in the Olympic Games, would be severely restricted by South Africa's distance from the big events in Europe, also keeping him out of view of the Great Britain team selectors – to say nothing of the country's apartheid system. The IOC banned South Africa from competing in the Olympic Games between 1964 and 1988. The Sturgess family returned to live in the UK, where they set up in Leicester to give Colin access to the city's old Saffron Lane Velodrome.

The Second Wave

Sturgess quickly made a name for himself in the UK, gaining selection for the 1986 Commonwealth Games, where the seventeen-year-old took the silver medal in the individual pursuit ahead of Chris Boardman. Sturgess was still a junior racer and his prospects looked fabulous. After winning several national titles and setting some very fast British records, Sturgess was selected for the 1988 Olympic Games in South Korea, where he finished fourth in the individual pursuit.

He turned professional after the Games, and in 1989 raced for the Belgian ADR team. The team was quite chaotic at times, but it was stuffed with talent. Classics winners Eddy Planckaert, Fons De Wolf and a young Johan Musseeuw were the team's top single-day race riders. It was also the only team to offer a place to the 1986 Tour de France winner Greg LeMond, who had spent the previous two years trying and failing to return to his former level after being shot in a freak hunting accident. He did return with ADR, winning very big indeed, which gained the team huge publicity, although LeMond's contract took up most of the team's budget. His deal with ADR was based on the American taking a fairly low salary, with massive bonuses if he won the Tour de France or the road race world title. ADR must have thought its money was quite safe, but he won both. The bonuses severely weakened the team's finances going forwards.

Sturgess was considered too young and inexperienced to be part of the 1989 ADR Tour de France team with LeMond, so he returned to Leicester to train for the 1989 track world championships in France, where he would compete in his old discipline of the individual pursuit.

There was something of the showman about the way Colin Sturgess raced a pursuit match. He was a very fast rider, as well as a strong one, and he used his speed to advantage in pursuit races. Most riders try to set an even pace through the entire distance of a pursuit, but Sturgess would hold back slightly at first then increase his pace towards the end, especially during the last lap. It was a tactic that involved impeccable pace judgement and self-knowledge, and it worked best on the big, four-hundred-metre-plus open-air velodromes, where the track world championships were most often held in those days.

In the final of the 1989 professional pursuit championships Sturgess was a full second behind his rival, Dean Woods, at the start of the last lap, but a blistering finish saw him pull that second back and add another 1.6 seconds to win the world title. It was very impressive, and exciting to watch.

Sturgess continued riding for the ADR team in 1990, winning the British professional road race title and doing well enough in Europe to get a place in the Dutch Tulip Computers team. That was a much more stable and better organised team than ADR, and should have been an opportunity for Sturgess to further his career, but it didn't happen. This is what he told me about that period:

'There was a lot going on pro cycling. It was the start of the nineties, the start of the EPO years [a drug for patients who aren't producing enough red blood cells – it increases the blood's oxygen-carrying capacity, which can be used to increase power for pedalling a bike], and EPO was a real performance enhancer. It made riders faster, simple as that. There were other drugs too. I wasn't going down that road, but what some other riders were doing started to get inside my head. The big moment, though, came at the track world championships that year. I qualified fastest, setting a new world record. I was in the track centre getting ready for the next round when a guy who worked for another team came up to me and said, "You won't win." I said, "Why not? I'm the fastest," but he just grinned. And I didn't win, I was beaten in the semi-final and ended up with the bronze medal, and that just cracked me up.'

◔ The Second Wave

Sturgess continued racing off and on for the next ten years. He had a year out to finish his degree in English literature in 1993, but came back to win a silver medal in the team pursuit at the 1996 Commonwealth games. He moved into sports journalism, becoming the editor of an Australian cycling magazine and stopped racing in 2000.

Chapter Seven
The Off-Roaders

The main off-road cycling disciplines are cyclo-cross, mountain bike racing and, more recently in the UK, gravel racing.

Gravel is too young a discipline for legends in the UK. Cyclo-cross is much older. Louise Robinson won a world championships silver medal and Helen Wyman and Nikki Brammeier did well at elite level in the 2000s. British men have only begun to make a really big impression at that level recently.

Instead, in this chapter we pay tribute to three very different off-roaders; one created a race that has become a British institution and was a formidable mountain athlete in his own right, the second was a top cross-country mountain bike racer in the early days of that sport, while the third was a huge force in downhill mountain bike racing.

John Rawnsley

7 April 1937 – 25 December 2019
Creator of the world's hardest cyclo-cross and an amazing mountain athlete

John Rawnsley conducting the prize-giving after the 2000 Three Peaks cyclo-cross

John Rawnsley was what the French call an original. We'd say a one-off in English, but 'original' is more picturesque, as well as a more fitting tribute to Rawnsley, a Bradford-born Yorkshireman who loved the picturesque Dales. Rawnsley worked as an accountant in the Bradford wool trade, but his weekends and evenings were spent cycling, walking or running. He was a good club road-racer, especially if a race was hilly and long, but he loved riding off-road and competing in cyclo-cross races, the cycling equivalent of cross-country racing in athletics.

By the late 1950s Rawnsley had walked the classic route, the Three Peaks in the Yorkshire Dales, many times – Ingleborough, Whernside and Pen-y-ghent, each of them topping out at just over two thousand feet. The walking route that links them is around twenty-five miles long, very beautiful, quite challenging, and is considered a rite of passage for hillwalkers.

A running race that follows the Three Peaks walking route was created in 1954. It is still considered a fell-running classic. The first recorded circuit of the Three Peaks route by a cyclist was Skipton schoolboy Kevin Watson in 1959. He rode the sections he could and carried his bike up the steep hills and where it was too rough or boggy to ride. Rawnsley read about Watson's adventure in the local paper and was inspired.

Starting in Ribblehead on a September Sunday in 1960, with friends Harry Bond, Geoff Whittam, Ron Bows and Pete O'Neil, they crossed Whernside first, then Ingleborough, then Pen-y-ghent in a total time of 4 hours 31 minutes 31 seconds. Rawnsley, who kept meticulous diaries, told me, 'We did it again in May 1961 and lowered the time to 3 hours 54 minutes. That was when I decided to organise the first official Three Peaks cyclo-cross on October the first, 1961.'

There were thirty-five starters in the first race and Rawnsley won it from Harry Bond. Everybody enjoyed it and so Rawnsley made the Three Peaks cyclo-cross an annual event. He would organise fifty editions and took part in most of them before letting someone else take over the complicated process. Landowner permissions to run the race took hours to negotiate each year – the route being mostly designated as footpaths now – so cycling is not normally allowed on them.

The Three Peaks is a wild cyclo-cross; it's over thirty miles long today and only the best can complete the course inside three hours. Many competitors take twice as long and more. More usually, cyclo-cross races are held over multiple laps of prepared parkland courses and they last around one hour for competitors at men's elite level, while other classes of competitors do shorter races. In the Three Peaks race, nobody is a stranger to rough cycling or hill running; it's not a fun event anyone can do. Entrants must prove their mountain race or other endurance credentials. Mountain rescue teams attend every year and quite a few rescues have been made over the years. Sometimes conditions are good, but even then the Three Peaks is still a very tough race. Sometimes conditions are terrible, with the risk of hypothermia or a fall and injury for anyone who underestimates the difficulty and on those days it's a struggle just to get through.

But for all its difficulties the Three Peaks inspires passion in participants, just as it did with John Rawnsley. Many take part year after year, and it attracts riders from all over the world. The race also attracts runners, because there are many sections where competitors have to run or walk, carrying their bikes. The world-class fell runner and cyclist Rob Jebb has dominated the Three Peaks in recent years, winning twelve times since 2000.

John Rawnsley took part in the Three Peaks cyclo-cross forty-five times. As well as winning the inaugural race he was often the first to finish in the various age groups he reached over the years. He also did the Three Peaks fell race thirty times and he often walked it, acting as a knowledgeable and very safe guide for others. By 2011 John Rawnsley had completed the Three Peaks on 152 occasions by walking, running or riding.

He was a supreme mountain athlete who was fascinated by off-road challenges. He was one of a select few to have completed the Bob Graham Round, crossing forty-two Lake District peaks on foot, a distance of seventy-four miles, within twenty-four hours. And in 1974 he set an extraordinary record when he rode the Pennine Way, 268 miles up the spine of northern England and into Scotland, in 2 days 23 hours 27 minutes. It's a ride that's strictly illegal now because it includes using footpaths where bikes aren't allowed.

John Rawnsley was the spirit of off-road cycling, a side of cycling that began soon after the safety bicycle was invented. His spirit lives on in the incredible race he created, the Three Peaks cyclo-cross.

Tim Gould

31 May 1964
Sole British medal winner in the UCI men's cross-country mountain bike world championships

Tim Gould takes part in a Three Peaks cyclo-cross

Tim Gould is famous for many exploits, including outdistancing a horse by bike in a cross-country race, but his substantive contribution to British cycling was as a pioneer in the early days of international cross-country mountain bike racing. Despite the sport's development, no British man has eclipsed Gould's performance in the UCI championships.

Gould, from Matlock, Derbyshire, was a good cyclo-cross rider, especially in the Three Peaks Race, where he was unbeatable in his prime. He was also a force in long, hilly road races too, and by coincidence a rider with similar abilities lived a few miles away at Matlock, in Dronfield, Derbyshire. His name was David Baker. They became teammates in the Ace Racing Team club, created by another local, Simon Burney, an ex-pro rider who loved cyclo-cross and the new sport of mountain bike racing. He later worked very successfully for its governing body, the UCI, developing both disciplines.

There is plenty of debate about where and when mountain bikes were invented – the same goes for mountain bike cross-country and downhill racing – but by the second half of the 1980s both disciplines were beginning to grow in the US and throughout Europe. In 1988 Gould and Baker rode their first cross-country mountain bike race, in Peebles, Scotland, where there is now a thriving mountain bike centre. Gould won with Baker second. Burney was at the race, supporting his two star riders, and he saw their potential in this new discipline.

'Tim and David were quite a few minutes ahead of anybody else so we decided to have a go at the World Championships that year,' Burney says. 'It was an unofficial championships, not under the umbrella of the UCI yet. The world championship races were held in Crans-Montana, in Switzerland. Two Americans – Mike Kloser and John Tomac – were first and second, with David third and Tim in fifth.'

The 1989 world championships were held in the America ski resort of Mammoth Mountain at an altitude of around nine thousand feet. Gould had already won a US cross-country mountain bike race at Big Bear, shortly before the worlds, so he was in good shape. There was to be a downhill and an uphill race, as well as the cross country at Mammoth Mountain. Gould won the uphill race and finished in the top ten in the cross-country, but Baker was quite badly affected by the altitude and didn't perform as well as he'd hoped.

In the same year, Gould took part in the 'Man vs Horse' challenge race held on a cross-country route in the hills around Llanwrtyd Wells, Wales. 'Man vs. Horse' is a headline-grabbing title, the brainchild of Gordon Green, the landlord of the Neuadd Arms hotel, Llanwrtyd Wells. The first Man vs. Horse race was held in 1980, and was initially a challenge for runners to compete against equine opponents. A horse won the first few editions, so in an effort to give human leg power a better chance, mountain-bike riders were allowed to compete in 1985, when Gould won.

The first official UCI mountain bike world cup series was held in 1990, and Tim Gould finished third overall. He also finished third in the men's cross-country race at the first official UCI cross-country mountain bike world championships, which were

The Off-Roaders

held in Durango. And to add to his bronze medal Gould won the uphill-only race at the Durango worlds.

There is no longer an uphill-only race at the UCI mountain bike world championships, so no British cyclist has had chance to repeat his feat in that. Gould is still the only British man to have won a medal in the cross-country race, although a present-day British cycling legend, Tom Pidcock, won the men's Olympic mountain bike cross-country title in 2021.

Steve Peat

Born 17 June 1974
First British downhill mountain bike world champion; sole British cyclist to have an iPhone game named after him

Steve Peat in action

Peaty clattering down a mountainside, is looking wild and out of control but in reality he is very controlled and precise... He's been doing it for years and is still a leading figure in the rarefied world of downhill mountain bike racing. Sheffield-born Steve Peat is one of the all-time greats. He won his first UCI mountain bike world cup race in 1998 at Snoqualmie in the US, and his last world cup in 2009. In between there were fifteen other wins in individual world cup races and three world cup overall titles. In 2009 Peat won his first and only UCI world championships in Canberra, Australia. It was the first downhill world title won by any British cyclist.

Let me explain the difference between UCI world cups and UCI world championships. World cups are season-long series, in which riders are awarded points according to their finishing position in the individual world cup races, or rounds of the world cup series. The UCI world championships in each discipline consists of a one-off race in which the world champion for the year and for the discipline is decided. The winner is called the world champion and wears a rainbow jersey every time he or she races in that discipline, until the following year's world championships. Most cycling disciplines have both a world cup series and world championships.

Peat's Australian world title was emotional, because he'd been in the sport almost since it started in Europe. The sport felt good about him winning – it was a just reward for his consistency and his friendliness. There was the same feeling in 2009 when Peat took his seventeenth world cup race victory, setting a new record for the number of individual world cup race victories. South Africa's Greg Minnaar holds the record now, with twenty-three individual wins.

Peat has done a huge amount of development work in downhill mountain-bike racing equipment, especially with protective clothing downhill. The iPhone game *Steve Peat Downhill* was named after him and he is a great advocate and worker for the involvement of young people in sport. He was also the subject of a biographical film, *Won't Back Down*.

Downhill racing is spectacular. It looks great on TV but, as with downhill skiing, you don't quite get the feel for the speed, or the steepness and difficulty of the downhill trails elite competitors race on from a TV screen. You need to watch in person to really appreciate how skilful elite competitors are. Most downhill mountain races are on tracks down mountainsides, but there are some notable street races, where riders negotiate back alleys, steps and the drop-offs found in hilly cities. Peat excels at those as much as he does in the wild. He's won the Lisbon downhill on the streets of Portugal's capital city an incredible eight times.

Steve Peat is a British cycling legend, but he also shares a birth date with the greatest male road cyclist of all time, the Belgian Eddy Merckx. Remember that, it could win you a round in a pub quiz one day. You never know.

Chapter Eight
Time of Change

British cycling started to change towards the end of the 1990s. Funding from the recently established National Lottery found its way into a number of British sports, including cycling, which used it very wisely. There wasn't much cash at first, but what there was gave the performance wing of British Cycling the opportunity to plan for success. There were still mavericks who went for it alone in this decade – indeed, this chapter starts with the story of a world champion of cycling mavericks. But by the early 2000s there was a structure in British Cycling to develop homegrown talent.

Graeme Obree

Born 11 September 1965
Maverick innovator, world champion, first modern British cyclist to break the men's elite World Hour Record

Graeme Obree at the 1995 World Championships

When Graeme Obree started cycling, he brought his own way of looking at things and asked questions, particularly about the way cyclists raced in individual time trials on the road and individual pursuit races on the track. He quickly decided that the way even the best did it, wasn't the best way to do it. He questioned everything – training, nutrition – but in particular bike design, and came up with his own answers, and as far as bike design was concerned his answers were faster.

From the late 1970s onwards, cyclists and bike designers became increasingly focused on the effects of aerodynamic drag, which increases exponentially with speed. This means that for every one mile per hour increase in speed a cyclist encounters many more times the drag they did when riding one mile per hour slower. As speed increases arithmetically, drag increases exponentially.

Cyclists always knew about the effects of drag and how they increased with speed – hence the dropped handlebars on race bikes, allowing riders to get lower and reduce the effects of drag. As cyclists pedal faster, they crouch lower, as they do when riding downhill. But this new focus on improving the aerodynamics of the cyclist began to change bike and clothing design, and new materials were introduced to the sport, like Lycra.

The two prongs of this new focus consisted of reducing the frontal area of the bike and rider package and of smoothing out the air flowing around and over it. The biggest part of the bike-rider package is the rider, and the biggest leap forward in reducing the rider part of the equation was the invention of tri-bars.

Tri-bars allow a cyclist to bring their arms and hands inside the frontal area of the rest of their body. That provides a much faster riding position because it lowers the body, which reduces drag and it reduces the drag created by the cyclist's arms. Graeme Obree took the aerodynamic drag-reducing effects of tri-bars two steps further when he invented two completely new riding positions. Both have since been banned, but they allowed cyclists to set records that are only just being beaten. Now much more is understood about how to train and prepare for top performance in cycling.

Graeme Obree was born in in Nuneaton, Warwickshire, but has lived in Scotland for most of his life and regards himself as Scottish. Scotland is where he took up cycling, competing in his first races towards the end of the 1980s. He rode time trials, but his unique mind quickly challenged the accepted norms of how to ride a time trial and how to ride a bike. The positions cyclists assumed with their upper bodies and arms, how they held their handlebars; none of it seemed to be the best way as far as Obree was concerned.

He quickly saw aerodynamic drag was the biggest limiter to speed on a bicycle and Obree's answer was to invent a new riding position that reduced the frontal area he presented as he rode, by removing the area occupied by his arms almost completely. It was similar to speed-skaters positioning both arms behind their backs when cruising in a straight line. He inverted a pair of standard road-racing dropped handlebars. That turned the flat bits usually at the bottom of the handlebars to the top, so Obree could both hold them and lay his upper body on them for support. He tucked his arms underneath his upper body, so his body was low on the bike and his arms were out of the air flow. The result was a measurable increase in time trial performance and Obree broke a lot of records on Scottish courses.

Obree's success got him wondering about where other aerodynamic gains could be made – not only from his body but from his bike itself. Working in his spare time in the backroom of his bike shop, Obree put together a radical new race bike. It had one fork blade – because one did the job of two and two meant increased frontal area, increasing drag. The bike also had a narrow bottom bracket which brought both the pedals and his legs closer together, further reducing drag. There were other innovations on the bike, the biggest being a set of custom-made handlebars that allowed Obree to present an even lower and narrower frontal area to the air he rode through, while almost removing drag created by his arms from the equation. He called his new bike 'Old Faithful' and began setting records on it.

In cycling, one record stands above all others – the Hour Record. It's mythical, mystical, but very straightforward in execution; how far a cyclist can ride in a velodrome in sixty minutes. The full title is the World Hour Record, but it's often referred to simply as 'The Hour'. Its mythical status comes from all the greats who have held both the men's and women's Hour Record. Its mystique comes from the fact that it is incredibly hard; so hard it has humbled some of the best in the sport.

Riding as fast as you can for one hour around and around a track, no uphill, no downhill, nowhere to ease, nowhere to change positions on the bike, no shelter, no pacing; just one rider, one bike, on one track, for one hour. It takes willpower, enormous physical and mental effort and deep self-knowledge.

With his new aerodynamic position on Old Faithful, Obree set about preparing to attack the World Hour Record and he trained

Time of Change

according to his own logical beliefs. Nowadays, anyone with talent is surrounded by coaches and is developed, brought on and has access to all the latest thinking in training, preparation, nutrition and everything in between. That wasn't generally the case in the UK in the 1990s. Even if a few chosen ones were getting help, Obree just did it himself.

Obree consulted all the physiology, medical and anatomy books he could and he saw the logic in one overriding principle of sports training: specificity. When preparing for any sporting challenge, the best training is to practise that sport, focusing specifically to improve the particular physical demands of the specific challenge.

The Hour Record demands riding at the fastest possible pace that can be maintained constantly for one hour and doing so on a cycle track while maintaining the most effective aerodynamic riding position for that person. Obree didn't have a handy track to train on, so he did the next best thing. His key training sessions for the Hour Record were spent riding as hard as he could ride for one hour, and no more, on a homemade, turbo trainer set up so that he could ride it in exactly the same position he used when riding Old Faithful.

Obree stuck to this idea of specific training session throughout his career. When preparing for individual pursuit races, his training would consist of a warm-up, then riding flat-out for five minutes, then pedalling easy to cool down and that was it. He did one such session in the morning and the exact same training session in the afternoon. This matched the heats and rounds of a championship pursuit series.

One hour flat out on a turbo trainer is physically and mentally exhausting and very few would-be Hour Record breakers would contemplate doing it once. They leave riding one hour at record place to the day of the event. Obree did it several times in the run-up to his records. He spaced out the sessions with several days of easy riding to recover, but that was how his logical thinking told him to do his specific training for The Hour.

And the World Hour Record Obree was training to break was a massive one; the 51.151 kilometres ridden by Francesco Moser of Italy in 1984 at the Mexico City Olympic Velodrome. Moser's distance broke the record set by Eddy Merckx in 1972, which was at one time thought to be unbeatable. He was helped by technical advances occurring between 1972 and 1984 and he trained specifically for the record attempt – he didn't just tack it on to the end of a busy road race season, like Eddy Merckx did.

And to really put the size of the challenge in perspective; Francesco Moser was one of the best professional cyclists of his generation, a world road-race champion, world pursuit champion, three times Paris–Roubaix winner, who would go on to win the Giro d'Italia in the same year that he broke Merckx's Hour Record. Moser also had a huge sponsorship budget and a team of technical and medical experts behind him. Graeme Obree was an amateur from Scotland who designed and built his own bike.

But that bike was fast.

Obree used Old Faithful to set a new British Hour Record at Herne Hill Velodrome in London, an outdoor track and in those days quite bumpy and not usually a place where records were broken. The bike looked strange, so did the way Obree rode it, but it was fast, although hardly anybody else could ride it, and certainly not for an hour. Those who tried it said it was quick, but it hurt their arms and their backs and they couldn't maintain speed on it.

But Obree could ride fast for an hour; he trained himself to do it. He also had a reason to do it. Well, two reasons. First, the World Hour Record fascinated him. Second, and more importantly, Obree thought breaking the record would earn him money quickly, and he needed money. His bike shop had gone bust, and he needed another stream of income urgently. His desire to beat Moser was ambitious, audacious and some thought it impossible, but Obree was determined. He says that when your back is up against a wall, you find strength from somewhere.

He convinced a sponsor to back him, got people to help, and with limited funds they went to the velodrome in Hamar, Norway. What happened next has become the stuff of legend. Obree tried on 16 July 1993, but failed to beat Moser's record by nearly a kilometre. It still meant Graeme Obree had ridden further than anyone else, even further than the greatest cyclist of all time, Eddy Merckx, but there is no second place in the Hour Record. It is beat it or bust, and it looked as if Obree was bust. Everybody else in the cycling world thought the same, except for Graeme Obree.

Nobody goes for it, fails to break the World Hour Record then gets right back up and tries again next day. But that was what Obree did; he'd booked the velodrome for twenty-four hours and couldn't afford an extension, but still had time left to go again the next morning. He was exhausted, his legs and arms seizing up from maintaining his extreme position for an hour. He knew that if he went on to go straight to sleep through the night he'd hardly be able to move the next morning, never mind set a world record. Obree drank lots of water first, which meant he woke up after an hour to go to the toilet. He then did some muscle stretches, drank more water and went back to sleep for another hour, after which he had to get up and repeated the process. He did that all through the night.

Next day, after a breakfast of Weetabix and milk, Obree broke Francesco Moser's Hour Record by riding 51.596 kilometres in sixty minutes. It was astonishing, incredible. The cycling world was stunned and many didn't know what to make of Obree. Had he broken an already amazing record, a record set by one of sport's the all-time greats because he was an all-time great, or was it because of his funny bike?

The European cycling press got another shock a few days later, when on 23 July another British cyclist, another British legend in fact (see next entry), Chris Boardman broke Obree's new record in Bordeaux, France. The pair shouldn't have been the kind of riders who set World Hour Records. The greatest road racers of all time, the likes of Fausto Coppi, Jacques Anquetil and Eddy Merckx set new World Hour Records, not a couple of time triallists from Britain.

The cycling media in Europe knew about Boardman from when he won the individual pursuit gold medal at the Barcelona Olympics in 1992, but none of them had heard of Graeme Obree. Then Obree won the 1993 world pursuit title at Hamar, Norway, beating Chris Boardman, as well as the established former world champion, Philippe Ermenault of France.

Some in the European cycling press tried to portray the two Brits as eccentrics who rode fast because of their freaky-looking bikes. Boardman had ridden the very futuristic Lotus carbon Monocoque bike to victory in Barcelona and a less radical – but still quite different – Corima bike when he beat Obree's Hour Record. But they looked like other bikes, Old Faithful didn't and it left the European press dumbfounded.

One German journalist called it the 'Devil bike', and a Norwegian newspaper said the world title had been won in Hamar 'by an eccentric Scotsman from a nation of inventors and explorers.' Another journalist compared Obree to Jan Boklöv, who revolutionised ski jumping by turning his skis outwards. They accepted Boardman, but didn't seem to want, or maybe they weren't ready, to accept a free-thinking maverick like Graeme Obree. He was never quite able to harness his talent as an athlete, or as an innovator, to make money from cycling.

Obree raced in the GP Eddy Merckx, a road time trial, in the autumn of 1993, but Old Faithful really only suited track cycling and didn't work on the twisting road circuit near Brussels. The sport's governing body didn't like the bike either, both on safety and aesthetic grounds, and eventually the design was banned from competition, but not before Obree broke Boardman's Hour Record, riding 52.713 kilometres on the Bordeaux track in April 1994.

Obree was making a name for himself by then and the sport accepted his physical ability, revered his determination, and his design thinking was widely applauded and copied. He wasn't about to stop following his own path. He started thinking about a new riding position that would give the same aerodynamic advantages and he came up with the 'Superman'.

Obree designed handlebars with very long tri-bar extensions, so the rider's upper body was laid flat with their arms outstretched in from of them. It was marginally faster than a standard tri-bar of the time, but not as fast as Old Faithful. Ironically, it probably suited the build of Chris Boardman more than it did Obree himself. Boardman set an incredible World Hour Record of 56.375 kilometres in September 1996 using the Superman position. That record lasted until 2022, when it was broken by Filippo Gana of Italy.

Sadly, for all his innovation and record setting Graeme Obree never found a regular place in a professional cycling team. A spell with a French pro team in 1995 came to nothing, and later the UCI banned Obree's Superman position. Cycling is very different today and Obree would have been appreciated and assimilated into it in the same way Dan Bigham has been by the INEOS Grenadiers team: Bigham started off as a maverick innovator, someone working outside of the system, but his talent as a rider and as an innovator was soon recognised. Bigham is a world champion now with the British team-pursuit squad, and runs technical development for

INEOS Grenadiers. That's what should have happened to British cycling legend Graeme Obree. His talent should have been recognised, valued and used.

Chris Boardman

Born 26 August 1968
First British cyclist to win Olympic gold in seventy years, second to wear the yellow jersey in the Tour de France, sole British cyclist to set three World Hour Records

Chris Boardman making his starting effort at the 1997 Porthole GP in the English Lake District

Chris Boardman is where the story of British cycling begins to change, and where this book begins to end.

Boardman was born in the Wirral into a cycling family – his father Keith was a time trial champion and Chris quickly showed outstanding talent. He also showed he was a thinker who, like Graeme Obree – his close rival early in his racing career – questioned the logic of the way things were traditionally done.

Once established as an amateur time trial star, Boardman met Peter Keen, an equally logical thinker, another questioner, a former youth time trial champion who was a university lecturer in sports physiology and a very talented coach. Together they laid the foundation underpinning the success of elite level British cyclists today. His influence in the success of British Cycling's performance team from 2000 to the present day is often overlooked, but is immense. He not only foresaw this success, he planned it. He became the performance director for UK Sport, where he masterminded the extraordinary overall British success at the 2012 London Olympic Games. Sport in this country owes Keen a lot – in fact, he's a bit of a legend himself.

Boardman was introduced to Keen by Doug Dailey, a former Olympian and the national coach for the British Cycling Federation during the 1980s and early 1990s. There wasn't much money for Dailey to develop riders when he did the job, but he tried, and he knew the best way to develop Boardman was to put him with Peter Keen, who recognised his talent immediately. It was in a branch of the sport in which Keen had based his doctorate, the individual pursuit, and he knew how to develop the new star. Keen and Boardman were kindred spirits: Boardman saw realising his potential as a challenge worth doing for its own sake, not because he wanted glory. He just wanted to reach a level of perfect execution. Glory might come if he did that, but it was secondary.

This is how Boardman once described their relationship to me: 'Peter wasn't interested in the history or mystique of cycling, but in looking at the demands of the event, breaking it down into its individual pieces then doing the training to meet those little pieces, and therefore the demands. I'm fascinated by how things work, including how I work. My background is in wood, so I'm into how things are made, and into measuring. Peter Keen gave me something I didn't have when I was younger; he gave me process and I became fascinated by it. I probably became more interested in the journey than getting there, to be honest.'

Boardman won his first senior national titles – the twenty-five-mile time trial and the individual pursuit – while he was still a teenager. He started doing more road races, and continued winning national track and time trial titles, going faster and faster all the time. There was no road time trial in the Olympic cycling programme in 1992, but Boardman's selection for the individual pursuit at the Barcelona Games that year was certain. What bike he would ride was less certain, and it is where the next piece of innovation in this story of British cycling excellence comes from.

While Chris Boardman's cycling career was in its ascendency, another free-thinking inventor was developing a bike quite different to those that racing cyclists had been riding. Bikes were made from steel or aluminium at that time, with some made from carbon fibre in tube form. Inventor Mike Burrows thought carbon fibre was the future for race bike manufacture, but he saw no point in using the material as tubes, when it could be moulded into any – more aerodynamic – shapes.

Burrows came up with a radical change in the way a race bike looked. He took his prototype to the cycle industry, but the response was it was too radical, until Peter Keen saw it. He approached Burrows with the idea of developing his prototype to suit Chris Boardman. Burrows had a friend who worked for the sports car manufacturer Lotus, who made the monocoque frame with no tubes at all, just in one flowing, aerodynamic shape. The British Cycling Federation took it to the UCI, which agreed it could be used in international competition. In 1992 Chris Boardman won the individual pursuit gold medal at the Barcelona Olympics riding his Burrows-designed, Lotus-branded bike, and both became famous overnight.

It was the first Olympic gold medal won by a British cyclist for over seventy years and with that box ticked Boardman and Keen started to prepare for another objective, Francesco Moser's 1984 world hour record of 51.151 kilometres. This was, coincidentally, the objective Graeme Obree was pursuing. In fact, Obree got there first, breaking the record in Norway a few days before Boardman was scheduled to go in Bordeaux.

Bordeaux was chosen not just for the speed of its cycling track, but because the Tour de France was in the city on the day Boardman went for the record. When he broke it all the world's cycling press was on hand to report it and he got maximum publicity. He was also offered a contract by the French GAN professional cycling team.

It was the first time a British rider had gained a place in a top European pro team without going to Europe as an amateur, living and racing there successfully and attracting a pro team through results in Europe. Chris Boardman is humble enough to admit he wouldn't have made it that way. 'I would not have survived going abroad as an amateur and living there for two years. It's such a dangerous path to follow; so many things can go wrong. I didn't even want to turn pro originally, but I thought I may as well try to move forward. If it didn't work at least I could go back to where I was before, so I had nothing to lose.'

The GAN pro team was run by an ex-Peugeot professional, Roger Legeay who, although he had as traditional a European background as any other team manager, was very modern in his thinking and flexible. Instead of expecting Boardman to adapt to his team and his beliefs – which is what all other Brits had to do in Europe – he knew the best way to help him make his way in top-level pro road racing was to listen to what he wanted.

Boardman explains what happened. 'When I had my first one-to-one meeting with Roger, the first thing he said was, "What do you want to do?" I said that in 1994 I wanted to ride a few races early on, then the [Critérium du] Dauphiné, then the Tour de France. But I only wanted to ride the Tour for ten days, then train for the time trial and pursuit at the World Championships in Sicily that year. Roger replied that we'd see about the Tour, because not many first-year pros get to ride it, but he was relaxed about everything else and he signed off on it. That became our process for each year.

'Luckily, I'd won the GP Eddy Merckx time trial for GAN at the end of 1993, because I struggled for a few months at the start of 1994. I had so little road race experience and suddenly I was mixing with the most skilful cyclists in the world. But then I did well in the Dauphiné, so I was selected for the GAN Tour de France team. The thing is I went to the 1994 Tour aiming at eight minutes and everybody else went for three weeks. I won the prologue time trial [this was the eight minutes] and got the yellow jersey, which was a

Time of Change

great return on investment for GAN. Plus, I won both the world titles I was aiming for in Sicily.'

Boardman's Critérium du Dauphiné debut was sensational. He won the prologue time trial and a longer time trial further on in the eight-day race. The longer time trial put him in the overall lead, which he lost when he was dropped on a stage with a mountain-top finish. But then he won the final road race stage with a tremendous lone breakaway.

Boardman's Tour de France prologue time trial victory was even more sensational. He won by some margin, completing the 7.2-kilometre course at an average speed well over 55 kilometres per hour, the fastest time trial average ever seen in Tour history – it remained the fastest until 2015. He was also the first British rider to wear the yellow jersey since Tom Simpson, twenty-two years before.

The 1994 Tour was joy for British cycling for many reasons. There was Boardman's yellow jersey, then Sean Yates wore it later in the race. Two Brits in yellow bookended the Tour's second visit to the UK. The first Tour visit had been during the 1970s – one quite uninspiring stage run up and down the new Plympton bypass in Devon. In 1994, there were two proper road stages in the UK; the first from Dover and Brighton, and the second a big loop through the countryside north of Portsmouth.

It would have been brilliant to have a British rider in the yellow jersey for the visit, but after defending for two days across northern France, the GAN team didn't have the strength in depth to keep Boardman in the lead during the team time trial stage that preceded the Tour's trip to England. Still, it was a magnificent two days in the UK, with millions lining the roads of Kent and Sussex to watch the Tour pass. As soon as the race returned to France, Sean Yates took the yellow jersey for a day. It really was like London buses – you wait ages for one, then two come along at once.

Boardman continued racing the 1994 Tour until the stage nine time trial, dropping out to prepare for the world championships in Sicily. With two world titles won there, he started looking at what else he could do in professional cycling and found another challenge he and Peter Keen could take on, take apart, see what it consisted of and then plan and execute training. It was a big one: they decided to target winning the Tour de France.

He set about a gruelling training schedule. Here's an example he told me about: one week in the winter of 1994/95 Boardman rode back-to-back eight-hour days. The idea was to lose weight and build endurance at the same time, but in the light of more recent discoveries, and knowledge about how to train, it was a bit of a sledgehammer to crack a nut. Physiologists, coaches and riders now know that Boardman could have achieved the same physiological changes in more precise ways. He also thinks, looking back, he would have been better with another advance in sports science and preparation that wasn't fully understood when he raced. 'I would have benefited from the psychological help that's available to athletes now. I was always a glass-half-empty sort of person. That meant I tried not to fail, rather than tried to succeed. It also meant I tended to avoid situations where I could lose, things like the national road race championships. I think my approach, my nature if you like, could have cost me some chances of success, and I think some psychological work could have helped me with that,' he says.

Unfortunately, Boardman didn't get chance to test his new training regime in the Tour de France. He crashed on wet roads a few minutes into the prologue time trial in Saint-Brieuc, Brittany, and sustained a shattered ankle and a broken wrist.

He came back to win the Critérium International in March 1996, then survived a brutal Tour de France. The 1996 Tour was particularly hard, not just because of uncharacteristic cold weather,

Time of Change

but because of what was going on in European pro cycling at that time. The average speed was in general very high, the top riders were doing things that seemed impossible, like riding up a mountain in higher gear ratios than anyone had seen used. The 1996 Tour winner, Bjarne Riis of Denmark, has since admitted using the banned drug EPO to boost his performance in the race. Jan Ulrich, who was runner-up, later admitted being involved in the Eufemiano Fuentes doping ring. Third-placed Richard Virenque and fourth man Laurent Dufaux were part of the 1998 Festina doping scandal.

There has never been any credible link with Chris Boardman and doping, so battling through to thirty-ninth place overall in that Tour de France did Boardman credit. It also did him good, three weeks of being dragged around France by several possibly souped-up contenders was three weeks of deep overload training. Boardman had a good second half to the 1996 season, with a time trial bronze medal at the Atlanta Olympic Games, when he was probably still tired from the Tour, and an astounding 4,000-metre pursuit world record of 4 minutes 11 seconds set while taking the 1996 world title in that discipline.

After that Boardman decided to capitalise on his super condition by trying to win back the World Hour Record for Britain. Graeme Obree's 1994 distance had been exceeded by Miguel Indurain of Spain, and by the Swiss rider Tony Rominger, who held the record before Boardman went for it again.

Manchester Velodrome was chosen as the venue, and Boardman decided to use the Obree-designed Superman riding position. A full house of 3,300 people witnessed something extraordinary in Manchester on 6 September 1996. The temperature inside the Velodrome was perfect and so was the air pressure, which is very important when setting records on a bike. High pressure means the molecules in air are closer together, which makes the air more dense, which increases drag. There was a near record low the day Boardman went for the Hour in 1996.

He started fast and kept it going, the crowd urging him on, the atmosphere was electric. Boardman has since told me, 'To get the right pace in a time trial, which the Hour Record is, you must keep asking yourself the same question over and over again. The question is, Can I keep this pace up for the whole distance or, in the case of the Hour Record for a whole sixty minutes, or whatever time is left? If the answer is "Yes", you need to ride faster, if it is, "No", you need to slow down, slightly, then ask the question again. The correct answer, the one that means you are riding at the correct pace is always, "Maybe".'

As Boardman entered the first banking on his 222nd lap of the Manchester track, a huge roar drowned out everything. A marker had been placed at that point in the lap before – indicating that this was where Boardman passed Rominger's 55.291 kilometres, and when he passed it Boardman still had sixty seconds left to ride. His eventual distance was 56.375 kilometres. The Superman position was fast, but so was Chris Boardman.

Boardman won the Tour de France prologue time trial for a final time in 1998 and got to wear the yellow jersey again. Then he had another go at the Hour Record, but under new and looking back quite strange rules.

The UCI banned the Superman position in favour of more standard aerodynamic riding positions using tri-bars – as well as other aero advances like disc wheels – for time trials and the track pursuit races, but they went further with the Hour Record. They went right back to 1972 in fact, reinstating Eddy Merckx's 49.431 kilometres as the new World Hour Record and said anyone attempting to beat it had to ride a bike that was similar in style and construction to the one Merckx rode.

Time of Change

The idea was to take the bike designer role out of record-breaking; a backward step. Nonetheless, Boardman went for the record again on a Merckx-style bike with standard dropped handlebars and spoked wheels, and rode further than Merckx when he set the record, but only just.

The new record was called the Athlete's Hour and Boardman's 56.375 kilometres using the Superman position was no longer the one to beat. But the Athlete's Hour was an anomaly – in the rest of international competition more aerodynamic bikes and riding positions were allowed. More extreme innovations such as Old Faithful and Superman were banned, but elsewhere others were not restricted to the same bikes and riding position as Eddy Merckx had used. It took a few years, but the UCI eventually dropped the Athlete's Hour bike regulations, and would-be record-breakers could ride bikes defined by the same specifications applied to bikes used elsewhere.

The Athlete's Hour was actually Chris Boardman's last competitive hurrah. He stopped racing but played a huge part in the British cycling success for which Peter Keen created the blueprint, the 'Performance Plan'. The Performance Plan was lottery-funded, increased with each success.

Lottery funding changed the way British cyclists make it to the top in world cycling. All riders in this book to this point have been marked by doing their own thing, and many were romantic adventurers. Now there is a pathway to the top, a well-funded system based in Manchester that has become a production line of champions, on the track, the road and eventually in the Tour de France.

When Sir Bradley Wiggins became the first ever British Tour de France winner in 2012, it was a victory planned by many of the same people who had planned all British cycling successes since 2000. Chris Boardman was heavily involved and now he's moved on to another major role in cycling. He is the man in charge of

Active Travel England and works to encourage walking and cycling as transport initiatives all over the country. He applies the same logic, the same questioning attitude to the job as he did with his cycling career and if his vision for Active Transport is realised, this country will have another reason to thank him.

Yvonne McGregor

Born 9 April 1961
First British woman to take an Olympic medal in the lottery funded era; World Hour Record-holder

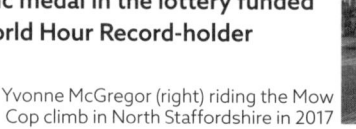

Yvonne McGregor (right) riding the Mow Cop climb in North Staffordshire in 2017

Yvonne McGregor, from the Wibsey area of Bradford, west Yorkshire, was a world-class fell runner until she was twenty-eight. She also competed in a few triathlons in the latter part of her running career, which ended because of an achilles tendon rupture. She stopped running for six months while she was recovering, rode her bike more, and was talked into riding a cycling time trial in October 1990.

More time trials followed in 1991, she got faster and, in 1992, took bronze medals in the British ten- and twenty-five-mile time trial championships. After that, still improving all the time, McGregor was selected for the England team at the 1994 Commonwealth Games and won the gold medal in the points race. It was a surprise, and an indication of her potential. McGregor had never ridden a bunched race on the track before. She had been told she would be good at the track pursuit races, so put in some practice on a banked cycling track before the Games, but all she'd ever done was ride around the bottom of the track, as individual pursuiters do. She never ventured up the bankings at all.

Lack of familiarity with moving around on a track made her tactics in the Commonwealth Games points race very simple. This is what she says about that early victory: 'I set off near the front of the bunch, riding around the bottom of the track and when the two riders in front of me had done their turn at pace-setting and swung up the banking, I just carried on riding, accelerating away from the bunch. I rode the rest of the race on my own like a time trial and led for enough laps to collect the points I needed to win.'

Winning that Commonwealth gold – beating far more experienced riders and doing so through sheer talent and strength – showed McGregor's potential. She was worth developing and was spotted by a man who could help her develop. Chris Boardman was a professional by 1994, but his personal manager, Peter Woodworth, still ran the cycling club Boardman belonged to, North Wirral Velo. It was sponsored by Kodak and by the 1990s had become a talent developing organisation as much as a traditional British cycling club. Woodworth invited McGregor to join the club, through which she met Boardman's coach Peter Keen.

Keen was impressed with McGregor's strength and saw she was perfectly suited to an extended time trial effort like the World Hour Record. He was dead right; some years after her racing career ended McGregor told me, 'If there was one thing in cycling I was made for it was the Hour Record, it suited me most. Internationally, there was the pursuit on the track, which is what I focused on later, but I felt I was better over longer distances. When I rode it the women's pursuit was 3,000 metres – so well under four minutes' effort – but I can just keep going. I always have been able to, when I was a kid they used to call me the "Duracell Bunny".'

In June 1995, McGregor rode 47.411 kilometres at the Manchester Velodrome, setting a new women's World Hour Record, beating the old distance by just under 300 metres. She was still an amateur when she did it, working to make ends meet and training in her spare time. It was a remarkable performance, and another marker of McGregor's potential. But the Hour Record didn't have the kudos for women it had for men, even in the 1990s.

Time of Change

Women's cycling was way behind men's in terms of support and sponsorship. It still is, but in these more enlightened times at least it's catching up. Today, breaking the record would have seen McGregor offered a place in a pro cycling team.

There were fewer teams then and those in Europe were focused on the continent. McGregor was undaunted and carried on working with Keen to make progress, but by 1997 she felt she had reached a plateau. She was training as hard as she could, but working full-time she wasn't getting the rest between sessions she needed to recover and fully benefit from her schedule. So she made a decision. 'I knew there was more potential in me and I wanted to see where it might take me, so I gave up my job and started to race and train full-time. I needed to do that to get to the next level, but it was really hand-to-mouth stuff. I was on the verge of quitting several times, and the only thing that kept me going was that I knew I hadn't got the best out of myself,' she says.

It was hard. McGregor told me about being in a grocer's shop and having to literally count how many pennies she had left to buy carrots. But that changed in 1998 when cycling became one of the sports to receive National Lottery funding. Athletes still didn't get massive amounts, but the best got enough to live on and at long last the performance side of various disciplines could hire professionals and buy or develop the equipment they needed.

Peter Keen had coached some of the most promising British riders for UK cycling's governing body, the British Cycling Federation, since the mid-1980s. He had been unpaid and was working full-time as a university lecturer. In 1997 Keen became the BCF's first performance director. He had a salary, a budget and some of the national squad riders received lottery funding as payments – only ten thousand pounds per rider per year and only for the best. It meant that all the top British competitors – mostly track riders, as men on the GB national squad who raced for professional teams were paid by those teams – could race and train full-time while living off their lottery support.

Keen introduced his World-Class Performance Plan (WCPP), which plotted a course towards long-term success. For this he drew on his work with Chris Boardman. A lot of the work Keen did was in the longer term, and it bore fruit after Keen had moved on, when Sir David Brailsford took over his role. However, whenever the story of British cycling success is told, Chris Boardman is anxious that Keen gets the credit he deserves. Boardman told me, 'When lottery money came, Peter implemented what he'd done with me on a wider scale. He also introduced the concept of a business plan for sport. The Performance Plan encompassed everything on a macro and micro scale. For example, it provided a method by which we looked at a rider's performance in a race, then looked at what they did the day before that race, then the day before that and so on, changing things, until by unpicking twelve months of training we could make a twelve-month plan going forwards that would reach a goal.'

Lottery funding changed the game from the day it and the Performance Plan were introduced, but at first there wasn't a great deal of money supporting the British Cycling team. More was available only for sports with proven potential to win Olympic gold medals, and potential was judged by success.

Knowing that, Keen spent the funds he had in the late 1990s on the disciplines of cycling he knew best, the track pursuits. He'd already coached Chris Boardman to Olympic and world titles in the individual pursuit, and Britain had individual pursuit world champions before. The country also had a good record at the Olympic Games in the team pursuit, with a number of medals over the years, although none since 1979.

Time of Change

For the 2000 Olympic Games in Sydney, Australia – the first for which British Cycling had lottery support – Keen spent most of the funding on the men's team and the women's individual pursuit. That caused friction. Pursuit riders were getting bikes that were custom-built for their races in terms of strength and aerodynamics, which were brilliant for pursuit racing, but weren't suitable for the sprint squad riders, which were so different they were like another sport.

Pursuit riders are endurance cyclists and have a lot in common with the way road racers train. In fact, endurance track racers use road racing as part of their preparation. Track sprinters, by contrast, are pure power cyclists. There is some endurance in their events, but they achieve full speed for a minute or less – much less, in the match sprint event. Sprinters put totally different demands on their bodies and on bike design. Even the aerodynamic and bike-handling demands of sprinting are different to those of a pursuit racer. A sprinter using a pursuit bike is using the wrong tool for their job, but for 2000 the GB sprinters didn't have sprint-specific bikes to ride.

Ironically, the GB track sprinters were the stars of the British team at the 2000 Sydney Games. Jason Queally won a gold medal in the 1,000-metre time trial and the Great Britain team sprinters, Queally, Chris Hoy (later knighted and an Olympic legend) and Craig MacLean, took the silver medal in the team sprint event.

For the pursuiters, the squad of Bradley Wiggins, Paul Manning, Chris Newton and Bryan Steel took a bronze medal and Yvonne McGregor won a bronze in women's individual pursuit.

McGregor went on to win the 2,000-metre individual pursuit world title a few weeks after the Olympics, but after a further year of top-level racing in 2001 she decided that the journey to explore her potential had reached its destination. Yet her contribution to British cycling in the years after she left the sport should never be forgotten.

Her Olympic bronze medal, alongside those won by other British riders in Sydney, meant that Team GB Cycling finished sixth in their sport's 2000 Olympic medal table and that was judged a success by UK Sport, the body that decides which sports get funding and how much they get. After the 2000 Olympics, British Cycling received more funding for its performance programme.

Sprinters got their own bikes – designed for the demands of their disciplines – and Peter Keen was able to roll out the next stage of his Performance Plan with more staff and he was able to focus on more events and that brought more success. More success meant more money and by 2012 cycling and rowing were the highest-funded sports in the British Olympic programme.

By then there was an established pathway to the top, and many have followed it. Riders like Sir Chris Hoy, Victoria Pendleton, Nicole Cooke, Mark Cavendish, Sir Bradley Wiggins, Dame Sarah Story, Geraint Thomas and, to a certain extent, Chris Froome have won the biggest races in the world because of the way the sport of cycling changed in the UK. They were the next generation of British cycling legends and many more will follow.

David Millar
Born 17 January 1977
The final British cyclist at the top in Europe pre-British Cycling Performance Plan

David Millar in 2014

David Millar was born in Malta in 1977 and grew up in Hong Kong. Like many before him he became fascinated by European professional road racing, devouring cycling magazines, poring over the pictures and reading race reports. He was soon enraptured by the stories of great riders in the Tour de France and other big races, and he became inspired. Ambition was ignited.

By the time he was a young teenager, Millar's parents were divorced, and while spending time with his mother in the UK, he started road racing and winning. By 1994, Millar was a regular member of the Great Britain junior road race team and took part in the 1995 Junior World Championships. He was also British junior twenty-five-mile time trial champion that year and all the time the lure of racing in Europe was growing and growing, until he had to act on his desire.

In 1996, and still only nineteen, Millar moved to France like so many ambitious British cyclists had before him. He was the last to make it really big before British Cycling's Performance Plan and lottery funding created a more certain pathway. Young ambitious riders still try to do it this way, and some make it, but the fact is the plan exists and it is a accepted route.

Millar based himself in St Quentin in northern France, racing for the local cycling club, where he won eight races, good quality ones. That attracted interest from five professional teams, including Cofidis, which was managed by Cyrille Guimard, who had a reputation for spotting talent. At first Guimard told him he thought he should wait another year before joining the European pro ranks. He thought that it might be better for him in the long run, better for his development, to do lots of national and international amateur races. It was a good deal: Guimard promised that Cofidis would still pay him his pro contract money, but Millar didn't want to wait. In 1997, at the age of twenty, he went full pro with Cofidis.

That was a big leap and the hothouse climate of top men's pro road racing during the late 1990s and well into the 2000s made it even bigger. It was a rough place for any young person. In interviews during his early pro years Millar talks about how he would take a beating in one race, recover, train hard, then get another beating in the next race. He even found his professional colleagues tough to train with. Reflecting on his pro debut now, David Millar says, 'Pro racing was far harder then than I expected. I didn't struggle at all as an amateur in France, but with the pros it was sometimes hard just to stay in the peloton.'

During his first Cofidis team training camp, Millar shared a room with a rider who openly took cortisone treatments – banned in cycling because they can be performance-enhancing. The rider told him that he felt under pressure from the team to take it. He was being a professional so he could do his job. Millar also saw evidence of EPO use within his team.

EPO was the drug of choice for a lot of pro cyclists and some other elite athletes in the 1990s and into the 2000s. EPO is used in medicine for those who aren't producing enough red blood cells. Red blood cells carry oxygen to body tissues, including skeletal muscles. If EPO is given to a healthy subject who is already producing enough red blood cells, it will still increase cell production. That increases the blood's oxygen-carrying capacity, which in turn increases the amount of power that person could apply to pedalling a bike. Used in this way EPO is the dictionary definition of a performance-enhancing drug: it gives measurable power output increases and that means a cyclist using it can rider faster.

Millar saw ice bags being delivered to rider's rooms, surreptitious behaviour from teammates, and defensive body language when they came out of the bathroom clutching little toilet or shoe bags, which they were careful to hide beneath other things. Millar reported his observations to an older teammate, who explained the ice was for storing EPO and the bags contained syringes and other medical equipment used to administer the drug. Millar was told EPO gave a huge advantage to users.

Doping had its own set of euphemisms; words like 'preparation' or 'recovery products' and 'good vitamins' and it was widespread in top-level men's road racing when David Millar joined the pro ranks, but it wasn't universal. Races were won without doping, and quite a few riders did win without enhancements. Millar had a great example in his own team, the Frenchman David Moncoutié. He won a stage in the Tour de France, four in the Vuelta a España, and was four times King of the Mountains in the Vuelta, and Moncoutié was generally acknowledged to be a clean rider.

Millar also wanted to race clean as a pro, and he did so for a while, but he slowly let go of that desire. He documents his fall from grace in a candid autobiography, *Racing Through The Dark*. He says he was clean when he won the opening time trial of the 2000 Tour de France, becoming the fourth British rider in history to wear the yellow jersey, but was slowly drawn into doping after that.

It's easy to dismiss doping riders from a moral standpoint, especially now it seems that top level pro cycling's attitude has changed for the better. Lots of evidence points to the fact that was not the attitude when Millar raced. Just say 'No', you might be thinking. But the thing is, when some ambitious, dedicated competitors with the ability and drive to win big can't reach the top because they are beaten by lesser riders benefiting from the effects of doping, joining the ranks is a temptation.

In my opinion, knowing what to do in this situation is especially difficult for young people and new pro cyclists are generally young people. They often haven't had much life experience, often less than their peers because they live for their sport. In such situations, many young people will take a lead from those around them. Especially more experienced people.

In pro cycling teams, that often means senior riders, and their influence is powerful if the senior rider is a person the young cyclist grew up admiring. They might also be guided by powerful figures around them, like team managers and personnel, coaches and even doctors working for the team. If those people are telling a young rider that doping is fine because everybody is doing it, or the team expects them to do it, or even that certain doping products helps them stay healthy while taking part in gruelling races; they are strong messages. And they are all examples of things I know young pro riders have been told in the past.

It's a very difficult world for an impressionable youngster to make their way in, or at least it was. There is a much greater duty of care within pro cycling teams now. Teams are also more committed to developing talent, a fact demonstrated by the long contracts some teams have given talented young riders. If a team invests lots of money over a number of years, it's not

Time of Change

in their interest to risk damaging the health of that rider, that 'investment', if you like.

I'm not making excuses for doping or dopers: it's wrong, it's against the rules of sport. It's also against the spirit of sport and the spirit of business. I just seek to provide some context, some background to show what was going on in men's pro cycling when Millar became part of it. A former US postal teammate of Lance Armstrong's, Jonathan Vaughters, explains the situation facing young pros in David Millar's era far better than me when he says, 'You either forgot your moral values or you forgot your ambitions.'

After deciding to use doping products, David Millar won a long time-trial in the 2003 Tour de France, and he became world time-trial champion in the same year. He also joined British Cycling's elite performance programme, run by Sir David Brailsford. Then something happened that removed Millar from those plans and changed his life for ever.

On 23 June 2004 Millar was having a meal with Brailsford in a restaurant in Biarritz, France, where Millar lived at the time, when Millar was arrested. The police were conducting an inquiry into possible doping within Cofidis and other teams and Millar had been implicated by at least one other Cofidis rider. The police told him he would be questioned, but first they were going to search his home in Biarritz. During that search they found two used syringes hidden inside books. Traces of Eprex, a brand of EPO, were found in the syringes and Millar admitted he'd used them.

Millar has said since that he'd decided to stop doping by the time he was arrested, but his arrest had consequences. He was stripped of his 2003 time-trial world title and he was banned from cycling for two years. Legal ramifications from the doping enquiry cost him a lot of money, but Brailsford kept faith. As a convicted doper Millar couldn't be selected for the Great Britain Olympic team, but he could be selected to ride for the British team in the world championships, where he made a great contribution on several occasions.

Millar also became an articulate critic of the drugs culture in top level men's pro road racing. He used his experiences to great effect when talking to young riders inside and outside of British Cycling's Performance Plan, those who were considering joining European amateur or pro teams, which the plan allowed them to do in order to get as much top-level racing experience as possible.

The racing experience those riders gained paid dividends when David Brailsford and British Cycling negotiated with Sky TV and formed Team Sky, the team that went on to win the Tour de France for the first time for this country with Sir Bradley Wiggins. Subsequent British Tour de France winners Chris Froome and Geraint Thomas were both team Sky Riders. David Millar helped set up the squad. One way or another he has contributed a lot to the British cycling story, both during his career and after it and his insightful TV commentary really helps us fans enjoy the sport.

Chapter Nine
The Golden Years

The 2000 Olympic Games saw British cyclists win more medals than they had for a long time at a single Games, but it was nothing to the golden flood that was to come. The first big British victories of this new millennium were in track cycling, but success there attracted more money from lottery-backed government funding, and especially from commercial sponsorship that led to the creation of a British world tour team. Within three years of that team's launch a British cyclist had won the Tour de France. More victories in the world's biggest road races followed, and many more will come.

Nicole Cooke

Born 13 April 1983
Britain's first Olympic road race champion, multi-world and Commonwealth Games champion and one of the greatest cyclists of her generation

Nicole Cooke winning the 2008 world title

Nicole Cooke is a force of nature. She is immensely talented – not just at cycling – uncompromising, strong and owes nothing to anybody, any system or coach. All she owes she owes to herself. She raced and won in every cycling discipline; road, track and off-road, and she was the best female road racer in the world during the early 2000s.

Cooke is from South Wales. She was born in Swansea and grew up in the Vale of Glamorgan. She is academically talented, achieving the best A-level results of any girl in the UK in her year and she was good at sport – and at one sport in particular she was brilliant from the start. She took up cycling aged eleven and at sixteen became the youngest person ever to win a British road race title at senior level.

She was soon racing internationally, winning four world titles as a junior (under eighteen) rider; two in the road race, one in the road time trial and she was junior world cross-country mountain bike champion as well. Her last junior world title came in 2001, in the era of lottery funding and British Cycling's Performance Plan, but Nicole Cooke was on her own performance plan.

She was a professional rider in 2002, moving to Forli, Italy, and riding for a part-Spanish, part-Ukrainian team. She didn't have to wait long for her first victory, winning top-level international races in Italy, France and the Netherlands that year. But the highlight of the year for this proud young Welshwoman was her road-race gold medal at the Commonwealth Games in Manchester. It was the first time a Welsh cyclist had won Commonwealth gold on the road (the next would be Geraint Thomas in 2014).

Cooke's debut in professional cycling was fantastic, but she came up against another reality of early 2000s pro cycling that year. It was in the women's Tour de France. She was struggling in the race, feeling below par and tired and she has recounted that her team suggested she take certain medicines to help her. She refused and the team stopped paying her. They even took her bike off her, and only direct intervention by the head of the team's sponsoring bike company, Ernesto Colnago, saw its return in time for that year's road race world championships. She left the team at the end of the racing season.

It was a good move, because in 2003 Cooke really got into her stride, winning three UCI World Cup races; La Flèche Wallonne, Amstel Gold Race and GP de Plouay, as well as the overall UCI World Cup title. She was also third in the road race world championships, but injured her knee in a bad race crash. The injury caused her to miss a month's racing in 2003, and more in 2004.

An operation on her knee in May 2004 finally solved the problem, but it was the end of June before Cooke rode her first race that year. She still won the Giro d'Italia Femminile, becoming the youngest winner of that race and the first British cyclist to win a Giro d'Italia, male or female.

Cooke was a phenomenon and continued as one of the very best cyclists in the world through 2005, reaching the top of the women's UCI world rankings the following year. Then she won the 2006 women's road race world title and scored another first for the UK that year.

I have already written about Millie Robinson and her 1955 victory in La Grande Boucle Féminine Internationale (which was meant to be a women's Tour de France but was actually restricted to Normandy); well, Nicole Cooke was the first British woman to win a real woman's Tour de France when she won a race simply called La Grand Boucle in 2006.

Cooke continued her domination during the first part of 2007, winning La Grande Boucle again, but another knee injury caused her to miss the world championships. She also lost the lead in the women's UCI World Cup that she'd held all year, finishing a narrow second to Marianne Vos of the Netherlands.

The 2008 Olympic Games were held in Beijing, China, with the women's road race the first event of the Olympic cycling programme. No British cyclist – male or female – had ever won a gold medal in the Olympic road race, but Nicole Cooke changed that with an imperious solo victory in China. It was the first British gold of the Games in any sport, the first cycling medal and the prelude to a landmark British Olympic cycling performance. Team GB Cycling finished on top of the cycling medals table, with eight golds, four silver medals and two bronze.

The Performance Plan had paid off, but I believe Nicole Cooke would have won with or without it. The sport changed during her career with a pathway to the top created by the lottery-funded efforts of British Cycling, with resources, coaches and an excellent talent finding process. Yet Nicole Cooke followed her own pathway. Later in 2008, she became the first cyclist ever, male or female, and from any country, to win the Olympic road race title and the road race world title in the same year. It was a fantastic time for British cycling, and for Cooke. She won the *Trans World Sport* female athlete of the year and the *Sunday Times* sportswoman of the year awards, and continued racing with great success until 2012.

She's been very active since, and vocal. She has spoken out against doping and sexism in cycling and was very candid about both problems in her award-winning autobiography, *The Breakaway*. She also presented a withering picture of the sport during the press conference when she announced she would stop racing. It made quite a few people feel uncomfortable, and it was quite right that they did too.

In 2017 Cooke gave written and oral evidence to the Parliamentary Select Committee for Culture, Media and Sport inquiry into combating doping in sport. Among other things she told the committee that information she had given to UK Anti-Doping (UKAD) hadn't been investigated. And she spoke about the sexism she encountered in cycling.

All in all, Cooke's evidence didn't present a very pretty picture, and it was brave and noble for her to do that. I think it's a great shame she isn't working in the sport today, which possibly shows that, although great strides have been made to make elite level cycling a cleaner and healthier place to be for young people, there is much more work to do. Nicole Cooke can help, but hopefully one day that work will be done.

Sir Chris Hoy

Born: 23 March 1976
Six-time Olympic and eleven-time world champion across four different track sprint disciplines; the most successful track racer of all time

Chris Hoy with his gold medals from the Beijing Olympics

Sir Chris Hoy is not just a British cycling legend, he is one of the legends of all British sport. He was the most successful British Olympian and the most successful Olympic cyclist ever between 2012 and 2021. Those records have now been taken by another British cycling legend, Jason Kenny, but Hoy's total championship haul means he is still the most successful track racer of all time.

Christopher Andrew Hoy was born in Edinburgh and grew up in its Murrayfield suburb. He was good academically and graduated from Edinburgh University with an honours degree in sports science, and he was very good at sport. He played rugby for his school and he was a gifted rower who was second in the 1993 British rowing championships in the coxless pairs, but performance excellence came on two wheels, and from a very early age.

Hoy started BMX racing aged seven, competing internationally for the next seven years. BMX is an explosive sprint discipline and at fourteen Hoy joined the Dunedin Cycling Club and tried several different cycling disciplines. Having watched his compatriot Eddie Alexander on TV taking the bronze medal in the sprint at the 1986 Commonwealth Games, when Hoy was ten, provided the inspiration for him to take up his true calling and he decided to try track cycling.

He left Dunedin to join City of Edinburgh Racing Club in 1997, based at the city's Meadowbank Velodrome and a real force in British track racing. One of Hoy's new club mates was Craig MacLean; they were both natural sprinters and kindred spirits. They made a quick impression on the sport nationally, winning titles and they trained together a lot and were quite innovative in their training, bouncing ideas off each other.

The sprint disciplines are very different to the rest of cycling. Sprinting places very different demands on cyclists, and sprinters train in a very different way to endurance riders. Explosive power and muscular grunt are of prime importance, and they are addressed by sprinters when they train on their bikes and, in particular, when they train off the bike. No cyclist spends as much time on strength and conditioning as track sprinters do, focusing on heavy weight training. Hoy and MacLean both did sessions in the gym, but they also used their bike training to build muscular strength. Here's what Hoy told me about one of the more extreme training sessions they thought up together. 'We used to do hill repeats – riding up and down a hill near Edinburgh airport. He did them on heavy, fixed-gear training bikes that we added weights to. Craig even put weight-lifting discs in the pannier bags of his bike, so it weighed over forty kilograms. We rode up and down that hill giving it everything we could, sometimes pedalling with the front brake applied to provide even more resistance to push against.'

The training brought results and their results brought them places in the British cycling team. Hoy and MacLean were one of the three British riders who took a team sprint silver medal at the 1999 world championships in Berlin. They followed that with silver in the team sprint at the 2000 Sydney Olympics. It was the start of a golden period for British cycling and for Chris Hoy in particular.

Hoy's sprint isn't just a short explosive effort; it's a long burst of fearsome speed and looking at the 2004 Olympic Games, Hoy decided to target the 1,000-metre time trial. The event is no longer part of the Olympics, although it is still part of every world championships. It's an incredibly demanding race in which – because of the size and nature of their muscles – sprinters create huge amounts of lactate, which floods into their blood – and it hurts. An endurance rider cannot produce anything like the lactate a sprinter can, so they never feel this unique pain, pain that Hoy likens to, 'Having red-hot barbed wire pulled through your veins'.

To address the requirements, although unfortunately not the pain, Hoy did a regular and very brutal lactate-tolerance training session. Each one saw him writhing in pain on the floor afterwards, and he did them on a regular basis throughout each four-year Olympic cycle, giving everything he had in every session.

I once asked Hoy how he motivated himself to train that hard on, for example, a dark Tuesday in November, three-and-a-half years from the next Olympic Games. His reply provides a window into the mindset of an Olympic champion. 'If I stood on the podium in the silver medal position at the next Olympics, but I knew I'd given everything I had in every single training session for the previous four years, I would stand there with pride and be happy. But if I knew there was a session I did, where I hadn't given a hundred per cent, I would be racked with regret and guilt.'

Mental discipline like that is the hallmark of Chris Hoy's career and it showed through again at the 2004 Olympic Games in Athens, where he won the gold medal he'd trained so hard to get in the 1,000-metre time trial. As the reigning world champion, Hoy was the last to ride the Olympic 1,000-metres, and three of the four riders who started ahead of him went faster than the old Olympic record. The rider immediately before Hoy, Arnaud Tournant of France, even set a new sea-level world record right there. All had gone faster than Hoy ever had.

To take the gold medal Hoy not only had to ride faster than ever, he had to set a new sea-level world record. That was a formidable challenge, but this is how Hoy dealt with it. 'I put the times in perspective by reasoning that the riders had gone fast because it was a fast track on a fast day, which is a rational explanation. Then I forgot about their times and focused on my performance, in particular on executing every separate piece of my effort optimally. I had practised everything, I just had to do everything perfectly. And then I did it,' he says.

Once the joy and celebrations around his first Olympic gold medal had subsided, Hoy targeted the next Games. The fact that the Olympic authorities took the 1,000-metre time trial out of their programme didn't affect him at all. 'I focused on the keirin instead. The best way I could race that discipline was by going for long sprints. It was an effort similar to the one used in the 1,000 metres, so the training was similar,' Hoy says. It proved very successful.

Hoy won three gold medals in Beijing in 2008, winning all the men's sprint disciplines – the keirin, the team sprint and the match sprint. It was incredible. Hoy was unbeatable, the master of sprinting for his generation and one of the very best track sprinters of all time. He was also incredibly popular, both inside and outside of cycling. The Beijing Olympics were great not only for Team GB cycling, but also for British competitors in other sports. However, it was Chris Hoy who was voted BBC Sports Personality of the Year. To top that, Hoy was knighted in early 2009, the first cyclist to receive the honour.

Hoy's career continued until 2012 and the London Olympic Games, where he was the Team GB flag carrier at the spectacular and very memorable opening ceremony, another first for cycling. His performances in the velodrome were no less spectacular, winning him the gold medal in the team sprint and in the keirin, a discipline he absolutely dominated during his career. Hoy had one keirin tactic – extended blistering speed. Everybody knew what it was, everybody expected it, he used it in every race and nobody could beat it.

Sir Chris Hoy is one of the most respected sportspeople of recent times. He was an incredibly tough competitor, but he always competed with great fairness and dignity. An absolute sporting gentleman and one of the all-time British greats.

Sir Bradley Wiggins

Born: 28 April 1980
The first British winner of the Tour de France and seven-time world champion

Bradley Wiggins in 2006

Where does a writer start with Sir Bradley Wiggins? He has won so many titles over such a wide range of disciplines, and he's won the biggest bike race on the planet; the Tour de France. Best to start at the beginning, I think.

Bradley Marc Wiggins was born in Ghent, Belgium, the son of an Australian pro cyclist, Gary Wiggins and his English wife. Gary Wiggins was good at his sport; he became a regular on the European six-day circuit, but he wasn't a good father or a good husband. He abandoned his wife and child when Bradley was two years old, and Bradley and his mother moved to London to live with her parents.

Bradley became interested in cycling at the age of twelve while watching Chris Boardman win a gold medal in the individual pursuit at the 1992 Barcelona Olympics. He loved it and started racing and dreaming of Olympic success. Then he discovered the biggest road races that professionals ride, and he wanted success in those too.

Wiggins joined the Archer Road Club in north London. His father had been a member during the 1970s and after proving his talent in several local races, Bradley's mother approached Condor Cycles, a famous shop in central London, with a view to getting some help for her son. Condor agreed to sponsor Wiggins, helping him with bikes and equipment. In 1996 he won his first British track title, the junior 1,000-metre time trial, and the following year he won the junior titles in the 1,000-metres, the individual pursuit, the points race and the scratch race.

In 1998 Wiggins won his first world title in the junior individual pursuit. He dominated junior track racing in the UK and was selected for the England team at the 1998 Commonwealth Games in Kuala Lumpur, where he finished fourth in the individual pursuit and won a silver medal in the team pursuit.

British Cycling was receiving lottery funding by then and in 1999 Wiggins became a full-time funded athlete, training with the British team in Manchester. He performed well enough to gain selection for the British team pursuit squad for the 2000 Sydney Olympics, taking a bronze medal.

British Cycling's endurance track squad uses road racing to help riders get stronger and build their endurance. It was the policy to allow riders to join top European professional teams, if they could, so they had access to the best road race competitions. In 2002 Wiggins became a professional cyclist with the French Française des Jeux team, and moved to Nantes in the west of France. He thought he would be living the dream, but new professionals weren't nurtured by teams as they are today. Wiggins felt isolated, living on his own in a tiny flat in the French city and became unhappy.

The 2002 Commonwealth Games were a welcome relief, and Wiggins took two silver medals, but at the 2002 world championships he finished fifth in the individual pursuit, which was lower than British Cycling (BC) had expected. He was still unhappy racing for his French pro team and living in France, so BC asked Chris Boardman to be his mentor. It wasn't an easy relationship at first; Boardman is an extremely logical thinker, whereas Wiggins was much more inclined to think emotionally. Boardman asked Wiggins to write out his objectives, along with the path he intended to take to achieve them. His first attempts to do this were returned by Boardman, covered in comments in red. Boardman relentlessly pointed out that Wiggins's plans wouldn't achieve his objectives. It was frustrating for Wiggins, but Boardman slowly and patiently changed the way Wiggins thought, until he started planning with logic. In the end, they forged a plan, and it was a good one.

Wiggins won his first senior world title in 2003, in the individual pursuit. In 2004, he switched teams to Boardman's Credit Agricole, a French pro team, and made more improvements. Credit Agricole gave him time and space to train for the 2004 Athens Olympic Games, and Wiggins won the individual pursuit gold medal, his first Olympic gold. He also won silver in the team pursuit and the bronze medal in the Madison with Rob Hayles.

Wiggins had arrived, his track career proceeding in great leaps and bounds, but he became increasingly frustrated by his experiences in top level road racing. He won a few European pro road races, and finished his first Grand Tour, the 2005 Giro d'Italia, but he became disillusioned because of the number of European pro riders who were still doping.

Things came to a head in 2007. The Tour de France started magnificently for Wiggins when he was fourth in the prologue time trial in central London. He made a long lone breakaway in a later stage that brought him a lot of admiration, before his Cofidis team mate, Christian Morini, failed a dope test and the whole team withdrew from the race before the start of stage 16.

Things got worse; the whole team was taken away by the police and all its members questioned, which really shook Wiggins. For a while, he forgot any ambitions he had in road racing, and moved his focus back to track racing.

Wiggins began training with renewed enthusiasm, it was good to be back with the British team based at the Manchester Velodrome, which was close to where Wiggins lived with his family in Lancashire.

The 2008 track world championships were held at Manchester, and Wiggins was brilliant, winning the individual pursuit, team pursuit and the Madison world titles. He decided to try to win the gold medal in all three events at the 2008 Beijing Olympics.

It was ambitious, especially since his Madison partner Mark Cavendish was riding the Tour de France just before the Olympics. Cavendish was already established as the world's best road sprinter of his generation, and a lot was expected from him by his team. Cavendish and Wiggins would also be the overwhelming favourites to win the Olympic Madison gold, so they would be marked by all the other teams, which added to the difficulty of winning a race as tactically complicated as the Madison.

Wiggins was terrific in Beijing, achieving his first two objectives by taking gold in the individual and team pursuits, but in the Madison the expected marking did cause them problems. They finished a frustrated ninth, and for a while there was a rift between them, each blaming the other for their loss. But Wiggins and Cavendish are good friends, so it didn't last. Earlier in 2008 Wiggins had enjoyed leading out Cavendish for the stage sprints in the Giro d'Italia, when they were both members of the T-Mobile pro team. That was something he would repeat four years later in the final sprint of the 2012 Tour de France, providing one of the greatest moments in British sport.

Once the Beijing Games ended Wiggins had time to celebrate, then reflect, and he decided to commit to road racing again. There were signs that the sport was changing after years of doping scandals, so he felt there might be a more level playing field. The first thing he had to do, though, was lose weight.

Body weight isn't really a factor for track riders, but it is when racing on the roads. Roads have hills and the determinant of how fast a cyclist can ride uphill is their power output divided by their body weight. It's impossible to exaggerate how important it is for professional road racers to reduce their weight as much as is possible, while building and maintaining their sustainable power output and, most importantly, staying healthy.

To address this finely balanced equation Wiggins started doing much longer training rides, while making every effort to reduce his body weight. He did it with guidance from dieticians overseen by health professionals. Not everybody can do this successfully, but Wiggins could. He was a different cyclist in 2009, competitive in races he'd never been competitive in before, such as the cobbled classics. He showed good form in the 2009 Giro d'Italia, using it as preparation for the Tour de France. When the 2009 Tour de France finished in Paris, Wiggins was fourth overall. He'd equalled the highest ever British placing achieved by Pippa York in 1984. In the aftermath of US federal enquiries into Lance Armstrong, in which it was proved that the American took banned performance-enhancing drugs and used banned practices to win his seven Tours de France and other races, Wiggins was boosted to third overall.

While all that was going on, Sir David Brailsford was negotiating with Sky TV in an effort to not only get them to sponsor the British cycling team, but to take an even bigger step and sponsor a British professional road race team capable of competing in the world's biggest races. Brailsford was something of a gambler and to tie up the deal he promised Sky a British winner of the Tour de France within the next five years. He didn't really know who that winner would be when he made the promise, but the 2009 Tour proved Wiggins could be a contender.

In 2010 Team Sky entered men's professional road racing with Bradley Wiggins as its leader. It also entered with a massive fanfare and massive promises – too massive as it turned out, certainly in that first year. The team underachieved and everybody involved realised they had to step up their game. The following year Wiggins won the Critérium du Dauphiné stage race in France, a good form indicator for the Tour de France. However, after a great start Wiggins crashed in the 2011 Tour, breaking his collarbone. Team Sky regrouped and rode the 2011 Vuelta a España, in which Wiggins and teammate Chris Froome were superb. Froome was second overall, Wiggins was third and they both moved up a place the following June, when the winner, Juan José Cobo, was disqualified for a doping violation and his victory nullified.

After a brief post-Vuelta rest Wiggins began training with renewed fire for the 2012 Tour de France. The route that year favoured time triallists who could climb. On his day, Wiggins was the best time triallist in the world and he'd proved during the 2009 Tour and the 2011 Vuelta that he could climb well enough to follow or at least not to lose too much time to the best stage race climbers when they attacked. All Wiggins needed now was luck, and 2012 smiled on him. All the planets lined up: Wiggins won the 2012 Paris–Nice, the Tour of Romandy and the Critérium du Dauphiné, all of them big, week-long stage races and all before the Tour de France. He started the Tour as a hot favourite and didn't disappoint. Wiggins took the yellow jersey on stage 7, won the time trial stage 9 and defended well.

Team Sky backed him brilliantly, although there was a moment in the Pyrenees when Chris Froome pushed too hard on a key mountain climb while setting a pace designed to prevent attacks from rivals in their group. Wiggins was distanced for a while, but Froome responded to instructions from the Sky team car and slowed down and Wiggins caught up.

The incident fuelled a bit of gossip about a rift in the team, but it was nothing. Wiggins was the leader and given the length of the time trials that was the right choice for Team Sky to make. As if to underline that point, Wiggins won the final time trial, then a united Team Sky defended his yellow jersey all the way to Paris.

Mark Cavendish was a Team Sky rider that year, and he was wearing the rainbow jersey of the reigning road race world champion. He was the favourite to win the final stage on the Champs Élysées, and to put him in the best position to do that, Wiggins rode on the front of the peloton for the entire final lap, going so fast nobody could attack.

Cavendish was right behind him, so we saw a British yellow jersey leading a British rainbow jersey around the famous central Paris circuit, then along the Rue de Rivoli, across the Place de La Concorde and onto the Champs Élysées for the final time. That was where Cavendish accelerated as only he could, and won the stage. It was wonderful, but there was more to come.

Wiggins had just become the first British winner of the Tour de France in its 109-year history, but always intended to also go for gold in the time trial at the 2012 London Olympic Games straight after the Tour. He kept a lid on celebrations for a week (and Wiggins loves to celebrate) and achieved what he set out to do. He won the time trial, so had a road gold to go with his three Olympic track gold medals, and his story didn't end there.

In 2014 Wiggins won his first and only road world title in the time trial, then had a serious attempt to win Paris–Roubaix in 2015 and 2016. He didn't win, but he really tried and he did well. He set a new World Hour Record in June 2015 at the London Olympic Velodrome, then returned full-time to the track, winning his fifth Olympic gold medal in the team pursuit at the 2016 Rio de Janeiro games. His career had turned full circle and he ended it inside the Kuipke, the famous Velodrome in Ghent, when he won the Ghent Six Day for a second time in his career. It was 2018, thirty-eight years since he was born in the Belgian city.

Knighted after his 2012 Tour de France and Olympic gold medal double, Wiggins became one of the highest profile sports personalities in the UK, but for some the image of his glittering career has been dulled slightly by a report from the House of Commons Committee for Digital, Culture, Media and Sport. It concerned an enquiry into leaks of Wiggins's medical record and into the contents of a jiffy bag delivered to the Team Sky doctor, Dr Freeman, at the 2012 Critérium du Dauphiné.

The report questioned a number of therapeutic use exemption certificates (TUEs) issued to Wiggins by the UCI. TUEs allow a competitor to use what would otherwise be banned substances in competition when there is a medical need. As such drugs can also be performance enhancing, TUEs aren't routinely granted. Unfortunately, Dr Freeman was not good at keeping medical records, which could have proved or disproved that the substances administered to Wiggins were entirely for his health. There were also rumours about the contents of the infamous jiffy bag, and again Dr Freeman's record-keeping wasn't up to answering the rumours beyond doubt.

On top of that, there were questions about some staff who had worked for Team Sky, in particular a Dutch doctor, Geert Leinders, who was at the centre of a doping case involving the Dutch team, Rabobank. And if that wasn't enough there was a case where testosterone was delivered to British Cycling's headquarters in Manchester by a UK pharmacy. There is no TUE use for testosterone. Dr Freeman said the delivery was a mistake, but again his poor record-keeping couldn't back that up. The Commons committee drew the worst possible conclusion; there was no direct evidence that substances had been used by Wiggins and/or other team members for doping purposes, but the committee felt they had been.

The Golden Years

Did Bradley Wiggins game the system to improve his performance or did he genuinely need medicine to preserve his health and allow him to compete safely? Was the poor record-keeping a ploy to hide another truth or accidental? In my opinion it's sad that these questions will remain as a footnote to Wiggins's glorious cycling career, both for cycling fans and for him. Wiggins has always stated his innocence and there is nothing other than those questions to indicate he's not. It's a bad situation for everybody concerned.

Victoria Pendleton

Born 24 September 1980
Double Olympic gold medallist
and multiple world champion

Victoria Pendleton at the Beijing Olympics in 2008

Victoria Pendleton is Great Britain's most successful female sprinter. From 2008 until 2012 she was the best sprinter in the world, winning two Olympic gold medals, Olympic silver and multiple world titles in all the sprint disciplines. To do it she had to regularly beat some fearsome and talented competitors.

Victoria and her twin brother Alex Pendleton were born in Bedfordshire. Their father, Max Pendleton, was a good cyclist, especially at the grass track disciplines, where he was a British champion. Grass track racing was Victoria's initiation into competition, when aged thirteen she rode her first race at the Mildenhall grass track meeting in Suffolk.

She progressed well, showing natural speed on various grass and hard tracks, and impressed British Cycling's assistant national track coach, Marshall Thomas. However, before she contemplated a career as an international cyclist, Pendleton wanted to obtain a degree, an academic qualification she could rely on for employment after becoming an international cyclist. She still raced with some success as a student, gaining national championship medals in several different events, but her attention was on her degree. She graduated in sport and exercise science at Northumbria University in 2001.

Cycling's governing body, the UCI, runs a cycling school at its headquarters in Aigle, Switzerland. The school has its own velodrome, and Pendleton attended the school between 2002 and 2004, learning a lot of skills and working hard in training. She was fourth in the track sprint at the 2002 Commonwealth Games and fourth in the same discipline at the 2003 track world championships, then did the same again at the 2004 world championships.

Pendleton's progress was steady rather than spectacular. She did well in the 2004 UCI World Cup, finishing second overall and winning the Manchester round in her discipline. But her first Olympic Games, Athens 2004, saw Pendleton take sixth in the 500-metre time trial and ninth in the sprint. That was behind her potential, but there were good reasons.

Pendleton later revealed in her autobiography, *Between The Lines* that she suffered from low self-esteem in the early 2000s. Those issues prevented her performing at her best in Athens. It was a bad time and David Brailsford, who was then head of performance at British Cycling, was so concerned about Pendleton he sent Steve Peters to Aigle to help her.

Dr Steve Peters is a psychiatrist who has worked in several sports, but is perhaps most famous for his role with British Cycling. Sir Chris Hoy has said that Peters was 'the glue that held the British team together'. Peters' understanding of the human mind, emotion and reason is vast, as you'd expect from anyone with his qualifications, but it's the way he communicates his knowledge that makes him so useful in sport.

His explanation of how the mind works is simple, logical and helps people rely on their own logic rather than on their emotion. Logic is where sportspeople need to operate when they perform – emotion can come later, after the race. Peters quickly identified what was holding Pendleton back and was able to help her release her huge potential.

She won her first world title in the sprint in 2005 and by 2007 she was the best sprinter in the world. At the 2007 UCI world championships she won the sprint title, the keirin and with Shanaze Reade she won the team sprint. That's three out of the four sprint titles available at the world championships. She was ready for the 2008 Olympics in Beijing, but it brought incredible pressure. The team has been so successful since the mid-2000s that merely being a member came with high expectations. It was time for Peters to intervene once more.

He would warn all his British team riders to not dwell on winning and only focus on the process of preparation. This has thrown up two mantras that became part of British Cycling's performance mindset: 'focus on process' and 'control the controllable'. No competitor can control what their rivals do or how they perform in a race; all a competitor can control is the way they train, their diet, getting quality rest and everything else involved in their preparation for a race. Of course, winning can be a consequence for getting everything right in preparation, but should not be the focus.

Pendleton did everything right when preparing for the 2008 Beijing Olympic Games. She broke personal bests on the track and inside the weights room. In fact, the then national coach, Shane Sutton, told me that Pendleton did far more weights work than she ever had before the 2008 Games and lifted heavier weights than ever before. The British backroom staff had identified that her slender physique needed strength training up to an event.

When Pendleton arrived in Beijing she was in the form and condition of her life. She was the fastest qualifier for the match sprint with a time inside eleven seconds for 200 metres. Later she said she hardly felt the effort. She was the fastest in the competition, but one-on-one match sprinting is quite tactical – quite physical, as two riders fight for the line and intimidation is a tactic used by many sprinters.

Pendleton's opponent in the final of the sprint competition, Australia's Anna Meares, considered her vulnerable to intimidation.

She tried to dictate the tactics in the final, riding aggressively, in close contact with Pendleton, to make her give ground, but Pendleton was just too fast for Meares and beat her for the gold medal. She was where she should be, she was Olympic champion.

Her rivalry with Meares continued over the next few years, and mostly her speed saw Pendleton triumph. She won sprint world titles in 2009 and 2012. Neither was easy; the Dutch cyclist Willy Kanis ran her very close in the 2009 sprint final, and she crashed in the 2012 semi-final riding against Meares. Meares won the next leg of the semi but was disqualified for moving off her racing line. Pendleton won the decider after a photo-finish.

That was Pendleton's sixth world title and she won her second Olympic gold in the keirin at the 2012 London Games. She then progressed to the final of the sprint competition, where she faced Meares once more. This time, though, she was relegated after winning the deciding ride, and Meares was awarded the gold medal. It was a controversial decision and was greeted with boos and jeering inside the velodrome. It was Pendleton's last race and she said the way it ended tainted the occasion. But she also admitted that in a way she was glad it was all over.

Victoria Pendleton was an incredibly talented cyclist, a superb sprinter, the fastest of her generation, but she found the pressure difficult to deal with. That she did deal with pressure successfully, even battling through dark times while remaining a fantastic role model, says a lot about Pendleton's character; far more than Olympic medals will ever say.

Sir Jason Kenny
Born 23 March 1986
The most successful British Olympian

Jason Kenny at the 2015 European Championships

Jason Kenny won an incredible seven Olympic gold medals, nine Olympic medals in total, and no other British competitor has ever won more. It's an incredible record, but only part of the Kenny family's Olympic haul. His wife Laura Kenny has won three Olympic golds, and she is still competing at the time of writing so could well add to their twelve Olympic medals in total. They are without doubt the golden couple of British sport.

Jason Francis Kenny is from Bolton, Lancashire. He was good at all sports at school, but found his metier when he attended a track taster session at Manchester Velodrome. He was fast and was invited to take part in the Future Stars series at the velodrome, a prelude to some big track meetings and a great initiative, as it got potential Olympians used to racing at big occasions.

Kenny ended the Future Stars series in the top ten overall, but the series was a mix of sprints and endurance races and Kenny was a sprinter. That's where his successes lay from the off, and during the 2005/06 winter track season he won his first world title, the junior sprint event.

He was a senior rider the following winter and competed as a Great Britain sprinter in several rounds of the UCI track world cup. By 2008, Kenny was one of the best in the world, winning a gold medal in the team sprint at the Beijing Olympic Games, where he was defeated in the final of the match sprint by his teammate Chris Hoy. Just four years had elapsed since Kenny first rode a bike on a track and now he was an Olympic champion and had a silver medal to go with his gold.

Kenny made great progress between 2009 and 2011, winning rounds of the track world cup, world championships medals and he won the keirin event at the 2010 European championships. However, it's hard to judge the progress of British track sprinters between Olympic Games. Olympic success is what gets a sport big money from UK Sport. Consequently, British Cycling puts most of its effort into the Olympics. Track training programmes aim for peak form at each Games rather than for the world or European championships. Even equipment developments are for the Olympics. After each Games, British Cycling's technical staff start again, looking for any advantage they can develop in the equipment their riders use. The technicians always come up with several developments that provide measurable performance gains, but they don't drip feed them to the riders. British riders get them all at once for the Olympic Games. The boost to their physical performance is one thing, but the boost to their confidence is also massive.

Kenny came into his own at the 2012 Olympics. He won team sprint gold with Chris Hoy and Philip Hindes, setting a new world record for the event. And he won the sprint event, the third Olympic gold of his career.

London was great for all the British team, but for Jason Kenny the 2016 Olympics in Rio de Janeiro would be even better. He equalled Sir Chris Hoy's 2008 achievement, winning all three sprint golds; the sprint, keirin and team sprint. He was at the height of his powers, unstoppable, just like Hoy had been in Beijing. Kenny also had six gold medals in total, the same as Chris Hoy. Could he go one better?

He could. The 2020 Tokyo Olympics were actually held in 2021, because of the Covid-19 pandemic. There were indications after London that the Dutch sprint team would be Great Britain's biggest opposition in Tokyo, and so it proved. They beat Team GB in the team sprint and Kenny didn't look to have the same form he had in London in the match sprint. He qualified in a lowly eighth place then went out in the early match rounds. He did make it to the final of the keirin, so he had a chance for that seventh gold. A slim one, and he'd need a tactical masterstroke to win it.

Kenny was obviously down on top end speed in 2021 – the match sprint proved that – so his only chance was to go for a long sprint and hope he would catch the finalists by surprise. Surprise tactics often cause competitors to hesitate and in a sprint event that can be enough to allow the attacker to get a gap and hold it to win. Kenny did it perfectly, and he held on perfectly too, winning by 0.75 of a second, a big margin in a track sprint.

It was a superb end to his career and in 2022 Kenny received a knighthood as Britain's most successful Olympian. Laura Kenny was made a Dame Commander of the Order of the British Empire at the same ceremony and they are now Britain's most successful Olympic couple.

Chapter Ten
The Wheel Keeps On Turning

In this final chapter we look at the careers and achievements of four legends who are nearing the end of their racing careers. Their racing will help ensure that British cycling legends keep coming. In fact, many of the present generation are legendary already, but they are beyond the remit of this book because they will achieve so much more.

Dame Sarah Storey

Born 28 October 1977
Britain's greatest Paralympian

Dame Sarah Storey in action during a track pursuit race

There are so many incredible cyclists in this book it's hard for one to stand out, but some still do, and Sarah Storey is one of them. She is a multiple Paralympic gold medallist and world champion in two sports; swimming and cycling, although she says herself that cycling is her sporting home, and it is where she's been most dominant. Storey competes at the highest level against able-bodied cyclists and beats them, as well as having dominated Para-cycling for nearly twenty years.

Sports statistics make dry reading, but I want to make an exception for Sarah Storey, because hers are staggering; twenty-eight Paralympic medals (seventeen of them gold), twenty-nine world titles (six as a swimmer and twenty-three in cycling), seventy-five world records and six non-disabled British titles. She's also competed at every Paralympics since 1992, over thirty-one years in top-level sport!

Dame Sarah was born Sarah Bailey in Manchester. Her left hand was damaged before she was born, failed to develop and couldn't function when she was born. Her schooldays weren't happy. She was bullied but she found her identity in swimming. She won two gold medals, three silver and a bronze in the pool at the 1992 Paralympics in Barcelona.

She switched to cycling between the 2004 and 2008 Paralympics because she was suffering from persistent ear infections as a swimmer. The transition was smooth: Storey had to ride bikes adapted for the difficulties her left hand presented, but she went on to win the gold medal in the individual pursuit at the 2008 Paralympics in Beijing. In a foretaste of things to come, her winning time would have placed her in the top eight of the non-disabled individual pursuit at the Olympic Games and she won the 2008 British individual pursuit title against non-disabled cyclists.

Competing with the best non-disabled cyclists became a big part of Sarah Storey's cycling career. She was selected for the England team at the 2010 Commonwealth Games, the first disabled cyclist ever to represent England at this level. In 2011 she was part of the winning Great Britain team pursuit squad at the UCI track world cup held in Cali, Colombia. At the time she was longlisted for Team GB selection for the team pursuit at the 2012 London Olympics. Being considered was a mark of the high regard in which is held as a cyclist and she absolutely dominated her events at the London 2012 Paralympics. She won the road race and road time trial, the individual pursuit and the track 500-metre time trial.

It's worth drilling down into those results, because they say so much about Sarah Storey, her application and her ability to overcome. Her lack of left-hand grip worked against her most when climbing on a bike or doing standing starts – accelerating from a stop. The standing start is crucial in the track pursuits and time trials, as time lost at the start is difficult to recover when up to speed. But standing starts involve transferring huge amounts of power through the handlebars, which Sarah has to do by jamming her hand into a space created on her specially designed handlebars.

When she started cycling this was a big problem in a pursuit, where competitors have around half a lap to get up to full speed. The nature of drag and aerodynamics means that time lost at the start has to be made up by riding faster later, which is big ask at world-class level. But Sarah worked on her starts, practising over and over, to such effect that not only was she able to beat non-disabled competitors to win British pursuit titles, but she was able to take a gold medal in the 500-metre time trial at the London Paralympics. That is incredible, because a good start is crucial in what is a sprint event of under forty seconds.

Storey continues racing against non-disabled opposition at the time of writing, helping to create her own team with her husband, international sprinter and Para-cycling tandem pilot, Barney Storey. Together they run the Storey Racing, a women's pro cycling team that has competed since 2017.

In February 2015, Sarah attempted to break the non-disabled World Hour Record. It was a tremendous effort. The existing record was set in 2003 by the Dutch rider Leontien Zijlaard-van Moorsel, who was the best female bike racer of her generation. Storey rode 45.502 kilometres in the hour, which was 503 metres short of the non-disabled record but set a new Paralympic cycling record.

Storey became the UK's most successful female Paralympian when she won the individual pursuit gold medal at the 2016 games and she continues to dominate her category today. At the Tokyo Olympics in 2021 she added three more gold medals to her haul, taking her to a cycling career total of twelve and at the age of forty-three she broke her own world record in the individual pursuit by a wide margin. She is now also the Active Travel Commissioner for Greater Manchester and a non-executive board member of the Department of Transport.

Storey has received a number of honours. The first was an MBE in 1998 for services to swimming for people with disabilities. She received an OBE after the Beijing Paralympics, and she was made a dame following the 2012 London games for services to disabled sport.

Dame Sarah Storey is a force for good in British sport, a fine example for young people and an inspiration to all of us. She has overcome many obstacles and done so with grace and remained as modest and approachable as ever. She's an incredible athlete and an incredible person.

Chris Froome

Born 20 May 1985
One of the greatest Grand Tour riders of all time

Chris Froome in 2023

Chris Froome shares fourth place in the all-time Grand Tour winners list, along with Fausto Coppi, Miguel Induráin and Alberto Contador. Froome won the Tour de France four times, the Vuelta a España twice and the Giro d'Italia once, giving him a Grand Tour total of seven. Frenchmen Jacques Anquetil and Bernard Hinault are above him in third and second places with eight and ten Grand Tour wins each, while number one is the Belgian Eddy Merckx with eleven.

Just let those names sink in. They are incredible company to keep, some of the best cycling has ever seen and Chris Froome, a disarmingly quiet and understated man, is one of them. And his story is as incredible as his position in the sport.

Christopher Clive Froome was born in Kenya, an African country way outside mainstream cycling. Unlike those around him in the all-time Grand Tour winners list, Froome grew up outside cycling culture. His family was sporty; his father played international field hockey and his two older brothers were accomplished rugby players, but Chris Froome was pulled towards cycling. He didn't know why, he didn't know anything about the sport.

How little he knew about cycling was illustrated when he joined his first cycling club in Kenya. Froome displayed talent and was a likeable enthusiastic teenager, so his club mates bought him a replica Tour de France yellow jersey to ride in. Froome thanked them politely and wore it with pride, but he had no idea what it represented in the sport.

Nevertheless, he felt pulled towards cycling and, after completing two years of a degree course in economics, his cycling successes brought him the opportunity to race for the South African Konica-Minolta professional cycling team. Froome jumped at the chance, left his course, and moved to his team's base at the UCI's World Cycling Centre in Switzerland. Now he was racing in Europe and on other continents.

He was on a steep learning curve but learning quickly. He finished second in the road race at what is called the UCI B World Championships and he won a stage of the Tour of Japan. He was also getting noticed by bigger teams, and by the director of British Cycling's under-twenty-three academy, Rod Ellingworth.

Ellingworth helped Froome get a place in the British-based, South-African-sponsored Barloworld team. Barloworld competed in most of the big races, including the Tour de France, and Frome made his Tour debut in 2008. He finished eighty-fourth overall, but finishing any Tour de France is good. Everybody takes their best to the Tour.

Ellingworth followed Froome's progress closely and when he took a British passport through his British parents, Ellingworth included him in the plans he was working on with British Cycling in 2009; the professional road race team, Team Sky.

I spoke with Ellingworth regularly in those days, doing interviews for cycling magazines and informally as well. I remember Ellingworth being very excited about the potential he'd seen during performance tests Froome did with British Cycling. 'Off the charts numbers,' was a phrase Ellingworth used. I took that to mean Froome's sustained power output was huge and that's the holy grail performance attribute for an endurance cyclist, especially as a stage racer.

When Team Sky launched in 2010, Froome was part of it, but his learning curve grew even steeper. Mistakes can be made and rectified at Froome's level of pro racing, but in the World Tour everything is magnified a hundred times and there is little room for mistakes. It's unforgiving but well-paid. Froome's excellent performance tests only heightened those expectations. Unfortunately, Froome didn't meet them consistently.

He did OK in his first year, but in May 2011 Ellingworth related that Froome was making mistakes in races. When they were pointed out, he looked like he was taking in the feedback but would do it again. To add to that, Froome's physical performance in races was very erratic; he wasn't performing consistently at the level his test results indicated he should be capable of.

By August that year, Team Sky was considering not renewing Froome's contract, although they selected him for their 2011 Vuelta a España team. To cut a long story short, Froome did brilliantly. He was amazing in support of team leader Bradley Wiggins, but was in better physical form, because Wiggins had only just recovered from his 2011 Tour de France collarbone break. Froome got ahead of Wiggins in the overall standings, and the Team Sky pair finished second and third overall.

The outcome of the 2011 Vuelta wasn't actually settled until 2017, when Juan José Cobo had his victory quashed due to doping offences. Froome was declared the new winner, and became the first British cyclist to win a Grand Tour. But that's an aside to the main story.

Froome's performance change was huge, assuring his future with Team Sky and making it a lot more lucrative, but the change also sparked some suspicion. No wonder really; cycling has a long history with performance-enhancing drugs. However, it was later revealed that Froome had been suffering from the parasitic disease schistosomiasis, which he picked up during a visit to Kenya in 2010 and was responsible for his dips in form. The revelation assuaged most of the scepticism.

Froome won his first Tour de France stage in 2012 – the mountain-top finish when Bradley Wiggins took over the yellow jersey. Froome played a key role in Wiggins keeping that jersey to the end and his climbing ability was enough to justify the belief by Team Sky that they now had two potential Grand Tour winners. With the 2013 Tour de France route offering more advantage to climbers than time triallists, Froome was picked as Team Sky leader, while Wiggins would lead a different Team Sky campaign in the Giro d'Italia.

Chris Froome dominated the 2013 Tour de France, winning by over four minutes. He was backed by a super-strong Team Sky, but he put in some incredible solo performances, including blistering attacks on Mont Ventoux when he won the stage that finished at the top.

With his first Tour de France victory achieved, and with Bradley Wiggins focusing on different objectives, it looked like Chris Froome would contend again for the 2014 Tour. It started in the UK, but several crashes, some quite heavy, in the first few days put Froome out of the race. He had to wait for 2015 for his second Tour victory.

Froome rode very well, but his rags to riches rise was still being treated with suspicion by some. Team Sky tried to mitigate the situation by releasing some of his power file data from stages and, of course, as the winner, Froome was tested for doping more times than any other competitor – with no adverse findings. Later in his career, Froome underwent independent performance testing which was scrutinised by a third-party sports scientist, and nothing untoward was found.

Froome was suffering in the wake of the disillusionment that many cycling fans felt when the truth and extent of Lance Armstrong's doping were revealed at 2013. It was at the time of Froome's ascendency and he was caught in the crossfire of anger directed at Armstrong and others of his generation. I think the dignified, tolerant and always polite way Chris Froome dealt with this situation does him credit. He certainly didn't let it affect his cycling performance.

Froome won his third Tour de France in 2016. Team Sky was excellent at protecting Froome, often riding at such a high pace on mountain climbs that his rivals simply couldn't attack him. However, Froome has always either been able to create something dramatic, or something dramatic happens to him.

Both kinds of drama occurred in 2016. The first happened on a mostly flat stage 10 to Montpellier, and it was pure bike racing, a tactical masterstroke that caught out his rivals. Stages in this part of France are notorious for being subject to crosswinds, and cyclists use the effects to leave their rivals behind in a subtle but very effective way. Froome was aware of this, so was right at the front when the peloton hit the crosswind section with twelve kilometres to go. The Slovakian three-time road race world champion, Peter Sagan, attacked when Froome was very close. Sagan was a very strong rider and with quality help he could stay clear in these conditions. Froome put in a huge effort to ride up to Sagan, followed by his Sky teammate Geraint Thomas, who is a crafty, strong rider and quickly saw the potential of the move. It worked, the group stayed away and Froome gained time on his rivals on a day they least expected him to. It was risky: Froome was already in the yellow jersey and if the technique backfired he would have lost time.

There was more excitement the next day, only Froome didn't make this happen. On Mont Ventoux, one of the most dramatic places in Tour de France history, Froome was in the small leading group of three and, as they made their way up the mountain, the crowds thickened on the road to the point where a race motorbike in front of the Froome group couldn't get through and came to an abrupt stop. The three cyclists ran into the back of the motorbike. They were not going fast

The Wheel Keeps On Turning

enough to be hurt but where the other two riders got going, Froome's bike was broken and he had to run up the mountain until his team support car got to him with a spare. Froome swiftly got back into the race, but it was long enough for him to lose time. However, the race judges stepped in after the stage and annulled Froome's time gap.

Froome was at the height of his powers and in 2017 he achieved a rare Grand Tour double by winning the Tour de France – his third successive victory – and the Vuelta a España in the same year. It had been a long time since any cyclist did either of those things.

In December there was another dramatic twist in the Chris Froome story, when the UCI announced an 'adverse analytical finding' (AAF) had occurred with a doping sample he provided during the 2017 Vuelta, and he was mired in controversy again. At that time, competitors could use the asthma drug Salbutamol up to a certain level prescribed by the UCI, but Froome's sample was found to contain twice the allowed amount. A great deal of expert opinion was canvassed about the sample until July 2018, when the UCI issued a statement saying that it was satisfied the findings were not adverse, and Froome was allowed to compete again. Cue the next drama.

During the winter of 2017/18 Frome announced he would try to complete a Giro d'Italia–Tour de France double. His effort started badly when he crashed while warming up for the Giro opening time trial. Froome lost time straight off and was on the back foot. He went up and down the overall standings for ten days before maintaining an upward trend. At the start of the final week he was fourth overall and within four minutes of the race leader, British rider Adam Yates.

Stage 19 was the hardest, most mountainous of the race and Team Sky meticulously planned an audacious attempt to support Froome in a huge effort to get the time back and gain more to win the race. The plan was to put Yates under pressure from the stage start by riding hard, attacking and causing Yates's teammates to chase. The theory was that this approach would burn up Yates's men, and then Froome could attack, crack Yates and use the final two climbs to forge ahead alone and win the Giro d'Italia. The plan required pinpoint accuracy. Froome would have to be handed all the food and drink he needed in small amounts to support his gigantic individual effort, so saving him carrying extra weight.

The idea worked and it was glorious to watch, a perfect combination of total team effort, with staff and riders pulling together and with virtuoso physical and mental athletic effort by Chris Froome. I think it was the highlight of his entire career, and possibly the high point of Team Sky's story.

Unfortunately, Froome's chances of the Giro–Tour double was wrecked when he was involved in several race crashes during the first week. Typical of him, though, he pulled himself together and backed teammates Egan Bernal, then Geraint Thomas, who was the eventual Tour winner.

Froome went into 2019 intent on winning his fifth Tour de France. That would have pulled him equal with the riders who all have also won five Tours; Jacques Anquetil, Eddy Merckx, Bernard Hinault and Miguel Induráin, but it wasn't to be. On 12 June 2019 Froome was practising on the route of the time trial stage of the Critérium du Dauphiné, as most race favourites do, when he crashed at high speed. He sustained a fractured femur, elbow and several ribs and faced a long agonising journey to continue as a pro bike racer.

He has continued, but although he has shown occasional signs of the old Chris Froome, he's not yet been consistently good. At the time of writing, it looks unlikely that Froome will ever return to what he was, but he continues to try, remains in good humour and behaves with perfect composure. He's a great cyclist, a British cycling legend, but what a story, what a journey he's had to become one!

Lizzie Deignan

Born 18 December 1988
Britain's best-ever female single-day race rider

Lizzie Deignan in the rainbow jersey of world champion

Tom Simpson may have the best record of any British man in the biggest single-day road races, but Lizzie Deignan has equalled his tally of three monuments and a world road race title. She's also won many other classic road races, has by far the best single-day race record of any British woman and she's still racing. This tremendous cycling career came about because she didn't like maths.

Lizzie Deignan was born Elizabeth Mary Armitstead in Otley, west Yorkshire. She went to school at a time when British Cycling sent coaches into schools all over the UK, introduced volunteer pupils to cycling, got them to ride on a static trainer and invited any who showed promise to do more training with BC coaches. When the BC coaches visited her school, Lizzie was to have a double maths lesson, so she volunteered. She was already an accomplished middle-distance runner and when she also showed flair at cycling, the coaches invited her to join BC's training programme. She was on her way.

Deignan won a silver medal as a junior in her first world championships in 2008, then won seven events in the three rounds of the senior UCI track world cup during the winter of 2008/09. Her first world title came as a senior in the team pursuit in 2009 and at the same worlds she took silver in the scratch race, despite crashing, and bronze in the points race.

World champion on the track and still only twenty; in a few short years Deignan was an established part of the British cycling team, racing road and track. She was part the team that backed Nicole Cooke when she became road race world champion in Varese, Italy. British Cycling's endurance track racers have always mixed track and road, and in 2009 Deignan moved to Belgium and, racing for a Belgian professional team, took part in many top level road races.

At that time her big ambition was to represent Great Britain on the track at the 2012 London Olympics and although she won further track world championship medals she developed into one of Britain's best road racers. She joined the Cervelo Test Team and had more successes on European roads, as well as taking the road race silver medal at the 2020 Commonwealth Games in Delhi, India.

Her focus for London 2012 changed to the road race. Racing in Europe for a Dutch pro team – AA Drink – leontien.nl – Deignan won the Belgian spring classic, Het Nieuwsblad, then another, Gent–Wevelgem. She was one of the best in the Olympic road race, riding to a silver medal behind one of the all-time greats of women's cycling, Marianne Vos of the Netherlands.

Deignan was now one of the best road racers in the world and several pro road teams wanted her. Wisely, she chose the Dutch team, Boels-Dolmans, which at the time was the best in the business. However, prolonged stomach problems saw Deignan below her best in 2013. She made up for it the following year, her best so far. She won big European road races all year and the Commonwealth Games road race title. By the end of the road season Deignan had won the UCI road world cup, a mark of consistent top performances. And she was getting better and better.

That was proved when, after dominating much of 2015, Deignan became road race world champion in Richmond, Virginia. She was the fourth British woman to win that title after Beryl Burton,

The Wheel Keeps On Turning

Mandy Jones and Nicole Cooke. It was wonderful to see Deignan go on to win 2016 Het Nieuwsblad, Strade Bianche, Trofeo Alfredo Binda and the Tour of Flanders wearing the rainbow jersey of world champion. But so often in life glory precedes a problem, and before the 2016 Olympic Games, which was Deignan's number one objective for the year, she had to face a big challenge.

International athletes in most sports are subject to both in- and out-of-competition drugs tests. For obvious reasons no notice is given for out-of-competition, which is why athletes have to update the drugs testing authorities with their daily whereabouts and a window of time for when they could be available for a test, wherever they are.

If testers arrive at any such location within the timeframe specified but the athlete isn't available, that is recorded as a missed test. Three missed tests within a certain time means the athlete is suspended from competing, as they would be if they had provided a positive test. Before the 2016 Olympic Games it was revealed that Deignan had missed three tests and faced a suspension that would have kept her out of competition. She accepted that she missed two of the tests, but stated that the third was missed because of the testers. After a long, hard battle the Court of Arbitration for Sport (CAS) accepted her version and Deignan avoided suspension.

Deignan made a bumpy start to her 2017 road season. Illness interrupted her training, but she picked up in time for the hilly classics of late April and was second in all three. She then won the Tour of Yorkshire – a terrific win in her home county, where she still lives part of each year. In July, Deignan finished second to Annemiek van Vleuten of the Netherlands in La Course by le Tour de France, the latest embryo of a women's Tour, which finished at the summit of the legendary Col d'Izoard in the Alps.

Deignan married the Irish professional cyclist Philip Deignan in 2016, and in 2018 they had their first child. Returning to her sport in 2021, Lizzie took part in the delayed Tokyo Olympic Games, where she finished eleventh in the road race. She was disappointed with that result, but more than made amends by winning the first ever women's Paris–Roubaix in October 2021, after a long, daring, lone breakaway. It was a glorious victory; a combination of bravery, strength and fitness and technical mastery as she skilfully negotiated stretches of rough cobblestones that were especially slippery in the women's race.

Deignan took 2022 out of cycling to have her second child, but stated she will continue to race for her professional team Trek-Segafredo, at least until the end of 2023. Nobody would bet against her adding more victories to her outstanding cycling career.

Mark Cavendish

Born 21 May 1985
The greatest road race sprinter of all time

Cavendish wearing the yellow jersey at the Tour de France in 2016

For many years Mark Cavendish was the fastest man in the World Tour; the unrivalled king of the mass charge that is a World Tour race bunch sprint. Winning bunch sprints at World Tour level requires speed, strength, daring, vision and dogged determination; Mark Cavendish has them all, and more besides.

Like Dame Sarah Storey, Mark Cavendish is another British cycling legend whose career warrants a look at the numbers. He's won thirty-four stages in the Tour de France so far, equalling the record career total of Eddy Merckx. Cavendish also has ten stage wins in the Giro d'Italia to his name and he has won three stages in the Vuelta a España. His career total of top level professional road race victories is 186 and Cavendish is still racing. He is also the only British cyclist other than Tom Simpson to have won the men's elite road race world title, and the only one other than Simpson to win a monument; Milan–San Remo.

And there's more. Cavendish holds the British record for career total Grand Tour stages wins, he was the first British rider after Pippa York to win a stage in every Grand Tour. He once won seven stages in one Tour de France, which puts him second in the all-time standings for stage wins in one Tour; Charles Pélissier, Freddy Maertens and Eddy Merckx jointly lead that one with eight in one Tour. Cavendish is the only rider in history to win four consecutive final stages of the Tour de France on the Champs-Élysées. He's won the points competition in all three Grand Tours and the Tour de France green jersey twice, he's a double world champion on the track, and an Olympic and Commonwealth Games medallist.

I could easily go on: Mark Cavendish is a phenomenon in cycling. Especially when you consider that winning so much consistently over a long career in an area of cycling that requires split-second decisions, bravery, and exceptional nerve and speed, is remarkable. Which begs the question, why is Mark Cavendish so good?

He's a natural sprinter, which means he's probably got a higher proportion of fast twitch fibres in his muscles. I say 'probably' because his long-time coach, Rod Ellingworth says that's never been checked. Ellingworth explains why. 'He's fast, we didn't need to know anything else. Most of my coaching with Mark was to get him strong enough and fit enough to get to the end of races, where he could use his speed. That's what ninety-five per cent of his training is about.'

There are a few more reasons why Cavendish is fast, though and Ellingworth has also explained they are partly natural and partly coached. Cavendish likes to train with small groups of friends and, like many groups of cyclists, they sprint for landmarks. He's done that since he first started cycling; he practises his sprinting all the time. He isn't tall, and he sits very low on his bike, especially when sprinting, which means he creates less aerodynamic drag than bigger sprinters. Since aerodynamic drag increases at the square of speed, reducing drag is a big advantage at the 70-k.m.h.-plus speeds top road sprinters reach. He was coached by British Cycling as a track racer early in his career, so he learnt track sprinter speed techniques, such as keeping low and keeping elbows tucked in to reduce drag when sprinting. The discipline to do that has stuck with him.

Cavendish was born on the Isle of Man, where he was introduced to cycling. He loved it and his natural speed meant he was soon winning enough to attract the attention of British Cycling. Rod Ellingworth invited Cavendish to Manchester to be interviewed for the first intake of British Cycling's new under-twenty-three academy. He asked all the interviewees to describe their journey from home to Manchester in as much detail as they could. It was a question designed to test their powers of observation, an important skill in cycling. Mark Cavendish recounted his journey from the Isle of Man in such minute detail that Ellingworth was taken aback.

'Mark has amazing spatial awareness,' he told me. 'Not only can he can describe exactly how any bunch sprint played out, he will say things like; "I moved half a metre to my left with 150 metres to go," and when you play the aerial shots back, then freeze-frame them, he did move half a metre to his left and it was 150 metres to go. And he can do that for every sprint he's ever been in.'

Cavendish can also slow time down in his mind, which helps him enormously in the mayhem of a big bunch sprint. He says that what happens in seconds for us watching, and for other riders in the sprint, seems much longer to him. He can make decisions based only on what is happening around him at that moment. That allows him to see gaps opening that others might not see, which helps a lot when trying to navigate through the madness. It can also help him avoid crashes, of which there are lots in bunch sprints.

Mark Cavendish was remarkable, but he also forged a remarkable relationship with his coach. Rod Ellingworth understood him, he knew how to get the best from him, and he knew exactly what Cavendish's potential was. That allowed them to plan Cavendish's career, pick targets and hit them together. The 2011 road race world title was a good example.

The location of each world championships are known at least three years in advance, and in the case of road races sometimes the circuits are known. Ellingworth knew the 2011 worlds in

Copenhagen would suit sprinters more than any other type of rider. Cavendish would be at his best in 2011, meaning he could win in Copenhagen, and no British man had done that since Tom Simpson way back in 1965. They decided to make winning the Copenhagen worlds Cavendish's biggest objective.

But athletes working towards big objectives need things to aim for along the way, so Cavendish and Ellingworth decided to focus on another race only Simpson had won, Milan–San Remo. By 2009 several sprinters had won this Italian monument, and since Cavendish was the best of his generation, he could win it too. He started working with Ellingworth on trying to win Milan–San Remo in 2009.

It's worth drilling down a bit into the way they prepared for these two big races, because it shows how elite cyclists and coaches work together. British Cycling coaches break any race or discipline down into its constituent parts. They then formulate ways a rider can train to improve their performance at each constituent part, then they work on sustaining their performance through the whole race. In cycling road races it's hard to do, because there are so many variables. But Ellingworth did it for Milan–San Remo and for the 2011 road race world championships (as an aside, he once told me he had done the same for the Tour de France, three of four years before Sir Bradley Wiggins emerged as a contender).

One of the things Ellingworth had Cavendish do for Milan–San Remo was increase his track racing during the winter of 2008/09. That was to get him used to riding fast with lots of riders around him, replicating the early stages of Milan–San Remo. There are hills in the race which sprinters have to get over while staying near the front in order to have any chance of winning. However, apart from one pass early in the race, the hills aren't high mountains, and they are always taken at a high pace. To replicate that, Cavendish did a lot of training in the hills around his home in

Tuscany, with Ellingworth leading him on a motorbike, hitting the climbs fast. Once on each hill they practised different high-speed racing scenarios. Cavendish was ready and won his monument; Milan–San Remo.

There were two years to go to the Copenhagen world championships, where Ellingworth could see the role of the team would be crucial in backing Cavendish. National teams dispute world championships and the Commonwealth and Olympic Games, rather than commercially sponsored teams, meaning that Ellingworth had a big say in who would be in the team and the roles they played. He put together a long list of riders, but before he went further he needed them all to buy into backing Cavendish for Copenhagen.

He called his squad together in South Wales, outlined his plan and revealed that the name of their group effort would be Project Rainbow Jersey. Ellingworth went to the length of borrowing one of Tom Simpson's world championship rainbow jerseys from his family as a way of motivating his troops.

You will see the words 'marginal gains' used a lot about British Cycling's performance thinking, which doesn't just mean good equipment. It means turning over every stone to see if there is an advantage to be gained under it; physical, technical or psychological.

From their first meeting the team moved as one. In the world championships each rider had a role, and each executed it perfectly. One rider picked up any extra food Cavendish needed and took it to him. Two others had to pace Cavendish to the front of the peloton ready for the sole hill on the circuit. That way, Cavendish could make less effort on the climb than other riders, and even though he drifted back through the peloton he was always still with the front group at the top.

There were lots of other elements to preparing, most of them aimed at saving Cavendish's energy; Team GB needed the race to end in a sprint, and that meant stopping any breakaways. It was the job of several Team GB riders to set a high steady pace on the front of the peloton for that purpose. Bradley Wiggins rode the entire last lap on the front with such sustained speed that no rival could get away. Close to the finish, Geraint Thomas took over from Wiggins and led Cavendish into the final few hundred metres, where Cavendish delivered. He won the road race world title.

It was a great moment in a career full of great moments for Cavendish, but it was also a great moment for British Cycling and its performance coaches and staff.

Performance cycling has changed in the UK, and British Cycling has been the engine of change. Mark Cavendish is the last of our British cycling legends, and his story is the right one to close this book. He stands at the cusp of his generation of legends and those before him, and the next generation, when there will be many more British cycling legends for sure. I'm really looking forward to it.

List of Legends

Moore, James	3	Webb, Graham	91
Stanton, David	6	West, Les	95
Pilkington Mills, George	9	Engers, Alf	99
Bidlake, Frederick Thomas	12	Barras, Sid	104
Michael, Jimmy	17	Sherwen, Paul	109
Marsh, Dave	21	Jones, Graham	112
Holland, Charlie	24	York, Pippa	116
Stallard, Percy	28	Millar, Robert (see York, Pippa)	116
Fleming, Billie 'Dovey'	32	Yates, Sean	121
Godwin, Tommy	35	Doyle, Tony	125
Harris, Reg	39	Jones, Mandy	129
Gray, Eileen	47	Burton, Maurice	134
Sheridan, Eileen	52	Elliott, Malcolm	138
Robinson, Millie	54	Sturgess, Colin	143
Steel, Ian	59	Rawnsley, John	149
Robinson, Brian	63	Gould, Tim	152
Booty, Ray	67	Peat, Steve	155
Denson, Vin	70	Obree, Graeme	159
Burton, Beryl	74	Boardman, Chris	168
Simpson, Tom	78	McGregor, Yvonne	178
Hoban, Barry	85	Millar, David	184
Porter, Hugh	88	Cooke, Nicole	193

Hoy, Sir Chris	197	Storey, Dame Sarah	221
Wiggins, Sir Bradley	202	Froome, Chris	225
Pendleton, Victoria	211	Deignan, Lizzie	232
Kenny, Sir Jason	215	Cavendish, Mark	236

Picture Credits

Frederick Thomas Bidlake: Simon Speed; Billie Fleming: Fleming family archives; Charles Holland: *Cycling Weekly*; Jimmy Michael: Jules Beau; Tommy Godwin: *Cycling Weekly*; Eileen Grey: *Cycling Weekly*; Millie Robinson: *Cycling Weekly*; Beryl Burton: Author's own collection; Brian Robinson: John Pierce; Ian Steel: *Cycling Weekly*; Ray Booty: *Cycling Weekly*; Tom Simpson: Author's own collection; Vin Denson: *Cycling Weekly*; Gerry Cranham; Barry Hoban: Barry Hoban's collection; Graham Webb: Jack de Nijs; Hugh Porter: Michael Turnbull; Les West: Author's own collection; Sid Barras: John Pierce; Colin Sturgess: *Cycling Weekly*; Graham Jones: *Cycling Weekly*; Malcolm Elliott: Chris Sidwells; Robert Millar/Pippa York: *Cycling Weekly*; Sean Yates: Phil O'Connor; John Rawnsley: *Cycling Weekly*; Chris Boardman: Andy Jones; David Millar: Francis C. Franklin; Graeme Obree: Phil O'Connor; Yvonne McGregor: Chris Sidwells; Bradley Wiggins: Chris Sidwells; Jason Kenny: British Cycling; Mark Cavendish: Andy Jones; Chris Froome: Chris Froome; Maurice Burton: Charlotte Wilson.